Mars Hill Graduate Sch
mhgs.edu/libr

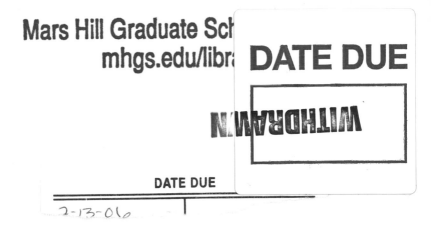

DATE DUE

WITHDRAWN

DATE DUE

7-13-06

D0312326

Rolfing Graduate School Library
ntegg.edu.Library

PREACHING RE-IMAGINED

The Role of the Sermon in Communities of Faith

Doug Pagitt

ZONDERVAN

PREACHING RE-IMAGINED
by Doug Pagitt

GRAND RAPIDS, MICHIGAN 49530 USA

Preaching Re-Imagined
Copyright ©2005 by Doug Pagitt

Youth Specialties Products, 300 South Pierce Street, El Cajon, CA 92020 are published by Zondervan, 5300 Patterson Avenue Southeast, Grand Rapids, MI 49530.

Library of Congress Cataloging-in-Publication Data
Pagitt, Doug, 1966-
    Preaching re-imagined : the role of the sermon in communities of faith
/ by Doug Pagitt.
        p. cm.
Includes bibliographical references.
ISBN-10: 0-310-26363-8 (pbk.)
ISBN-13: 978-0-310-26363-0 (pbk.)
1. Preaching. I. Title.
BV4211.3.P34 2005
251—dc22

                                                              2005002990

Unless otherwise indicated, all Scripture quotations are taken from the Holy Bible: Today's New International Version™, TNIV® Copyright ©2001, 2005 by International Bible Society®. All rights reserved worldwide.

All rights reserved. No part of this publication may be reproduced, stored in a retrieval system, or transmitted in any form or by any means—electronic, mechanical, photocopy, recording, or any other—(except for brief quotations in printed reviews) without the prior permission of the publisher.

Web site addresses listed in this book were current at the time of publication. Please contact Youth Specialties via e-mail (YS@YouthSpecialties.com) to report URLs that are no longer operational and replacement URLs if available.

Portions of text copied from Preaching & Preachers by Dr. D. Martyn Lloyd-Jones. Copyright ©1972 by Zondervan Publishing. Used by permission.

Editorial direction by Carla Barnhill
Edited by Laura Gross
Proofread by Janie Wilkerson and Kristi Robison
Interior design by SharpSeven Design
Cover design by Holly Sharp
Jacket photography by David Studarus
Author photo by Sarah Sampedro
Printed in the United States

---

05 06 07 08 09 10 / DCI / 10 9 8 7 6 5 4 3 2 1

TABLE OF CONTENTS

ACKNOWLEDGMENTS

With sincere heartfelt gratitude I want to thank the many people who have contributed to the creation of this book.

First to my family: Shelley, Michon, Taylor, Ruben, and Chico—I join you in being glad this book is done so we can get back to our normal schedule. Thank you for your gracious permission that allowed me to be gone or in the living room working on the book.

To the people of Solomon's Porch—thank you for allowing me to arrange my life in such a way that I could put energy into this project. My life is ever being changed by your participation in it. I love you all.

This book would not have been possible without the wonderful, brilliant work of my editor and friend, Carla Barnhill. Carla—thank you for your ideas, corrections, clarifications, and hard work. I mean it when I say this couldn't have happened without you.

Jimmy—thank you for sharing your wife and making it possible for her to give so much time to fixing my "ramblings."

Thom Olson—thank you for your contributions in the early stages of thinking through the ideas of this book. Your friendship is a treasure.

I would also like to express my appreciation to the good people at Youth Specialties—particularly Jay Howver, Mark Oestreicher, and Holly Sharp—and the folks at Zondervan, especially John Raymond, for your support of this book.

SECTION ONE
ANOTHER PREACHING BOOK?

I am sitting inside the Open Book writing center in Minneapolis on a summer day in 2004. My head is full of wonderings. I wonder who you are. I wonder what kinds of people will read a book about preaching in the emerging church. I wonder if I have anything to say on the topic. I wonder if I have written a single line of any value. I not only wonder, but I also worry. I worry about the opinions of people who don't think a pastor and author of a book about preaching should worry about things. I worry about people reading my sometimes-uncertain thoughts on preaching. I worry about coming across as someone who thinks of himself as an expert—someone who knows more than you and will tell you how to preach. So please, as you read, keep your worried, wondering author in mind.

I am a pastor who seeks to live in a community of people who are living out the hopes and aspirations of God in the world. Like many of you I play a particular role in my community. As the pastor I'm often referred to as "the preacher." And frankly, this is a role I no longer relish. There was a time when I did. There was a time when I felt my ability to deliver sermons was a high calling that I sought to refine but didn't need to redefine.

Those days are gone. Now I find myself regularly redefining my role and the role of preaching. I find myself wanting to live life with the people of my community where I can preach—along with the other preachers of our community—but not allow that to become an act of speech making. Instead I want it to be a living interaction of the story of God and the story of our community being connected by our truth telling, our vulnerability, and our open minds, ears, and eyes—all brought together by the active work of the Spirit of God as we "Let the message of Christ dwell among (us) richly as (we) teach and admonish one another with all wisdom through psalms, hymns and songs from the Spirit, singing to God with gratitude in (our) hearts" (Colossians 3:16).

If I had my way, this book would be a conversation about these desires. Instead of your reading something I wrote, we would talk over a meal or in my family room or at your house. We would hear from one another and build on what each other says. While a book cannot be a full conversation, my hope is that I will at least add to the conversation you may well be already having on preaching.

Please don't let the title of the book, *Preaching Re-Imagined*, throw you. I'm not prescribing a method for all churches of the future. In fact, I'm quite sure there is no *one* method. However, I am suggesting some deep considerations about the function and role of preaching within our communities of faith that will lead to particular practices—but these are not one-size-fits-all prescriptions. And in no way do I mean to suggest that I speak for all who choose to engage in preaching in the emerging world.

Throughout the book I suggest "*progressional dialogue*" (a phrase I made up) as a preferable alternative to "*speaching*" (another new word meaning "the style of preaching that's hardly distinguishable from a one-way speech"). In the spirit of dialogue I have designed this book to be as conversational and progressional as possible.

HOW TO READ THIS BOOK

The book isn't structured like a typical chapter book. It all begins in the next chapter where I lay out my basic premise and provide reference links to the 40 sub-sections that make up the last four sections of the book. Each subsection is designed to provide a more comprehensive discussion about a point I made in the opening chapter.

Section 2 is also loaded with statements that may cause you to say, "Hang on a minute," or, "You can't just say that without supporting it in some way." That's the intent. Much like a conversation where the participants push one another to say more on the topics in which they have an interest, the next chapter is meant to get the conversation started. That being the case, I have included reference numbers within the text of section 2. These are not footnotes but rather clues as to where you can find more conversation about a particular point in later sections.

From there you can either continue reading the rest of the book from start to finish, or you can jump between the points that interest you the most. For example, you might not be interested in the story of how I became a preacher but would prefer to go right to my suggestions on rethinking the role of the pastor. If so, you can skip point number five and go right to point 23.

I admit that part of my desire to structure the book in this way is to justify my own reading habits. I do this with books all the time—just skip around and read the parts that interest me in the order that seems most interesting to me. Sometimes I don't even read all of it. But I feel like I'm cheating or missing out on something by not following the prescribed order.

In this book, however, not only are you *not* cheating, but you're also *encouraged* to skip around as well. You won't miss out on something by doing so. In fact, I hope you'll gain something by taking the conversation wherever you want it to go. I've created a Weblog for those who wish to explore the ideas in this book with other readers. If you'd like to join that conversation, head to www.PreachingReimagined. com.

The book is also designed with more open space than usual. This is to encourage you to write your thoughts, to talk back, to not just sit there and take it. Put your ideas on the paper right next to mine; they belong there. In fact, they're needed. As part of the process of writing this book, I read a number of books about preaching. Over and over I found myself scribbling notes in the small margins—things like, "Yes, totally!" or, "No, no, no." But I felt like a vandal writing where my words weren't wanted, as if I was somehow defaming the book. On the contrary this book should not be left in its impersonal, published form. If it is, then it hasn't done its job of engaging you in the conversation.

So I invite you to continue reading this book with your dialogue hat on, a pen in hand, and an attitude of progressional conversation ready to go.

ONE MORE THING

I would like to make an essential clarification before we begin this "conversation." I will be writing with a basic assumption about the place of the church. It is my belief that as important as preaching is to the church, the goal of the church is not to be a "preaching center." Nor is the ultimate goal of the Christian faith the creation and health of churches. Rather , the goal of Christians, and of all of humanity, ought to be to join in the activity of God wherever we find it. That may lead to preaching, but preaching and church life are not the only way in which God is active in the world.

Our call is to live as what I like to refer to as "Kingdom-of-God Horticulturalists." In the same way a horticulturalist understands plant life, makes suggestions about what will thrive in a given environment, and knows how to nurture various forms of plant life, we are to recognize, encourage, and join God's always-growing work in the world.

The church is best understood not as the exclusive proprietor of all the things of God, but rather as the home base for those committed to living in rhythm with God. It is a means by which we extend God's hopes, dreams and agenda in the world, not an end goal in itself. Nor is preaching an end in itself but one of the many ways we as Christians ought to seek to tend to the things of God.

I am part of an organization—really more of a collection of friendships—called Emergent which has helped me understand and put it this thinking into practice in my life and our church. If you are intrigued by the ideas you find here, www.EmergentVillage.com serves as a gateway into these relationships. I encourage you consider joining us in the life of God wherever we find it.

SECTION TWO
PREACHING BEYOND SPEACHING

Despite the title this isn't really a book about preaching [1]. It's about more. It's a book about the kinds of communities we're seeking to become and the role preaching plays in the creation of those communities [25]. Preaching isn't an end in itself. We don't participate in Christian communities so we can produce and hear great sermons. We take part in these communities because we believe they're where we're formed and shaped to become the people of God—people who are actively living in the kingdom.

I'm writing with the assumption that most of you who are reading this book have concluded what I have: Preaching doesn't work—at least not in the ways we hope [7]. If it did, pastors wouldn't reach with such anticipation for new books about preaching; we'd already be following the established, tried-and-true methods laid out in the huge array of available preaching resources. We wouldn't have to preach anymore; we'd just replay our perfect sermons and watch our people change.

I believe preaching to be a crucial act of the church. That's why preaching needs to be released from the bondage of the speech making act [1, 4]. Our impulse to tell the story of God in our communities is the right one, but making speeches is the wrong way to do it. Our desire to be a people who is connected with the truth of God is the right one, but speeches won't get us there [17, 21, 22, 33]. This dependence on preaching as speech making has become a form of communication I call *speaching* [1]. Our desire to use our pastoral gifts of discernment, knowledge, and articulation for the benefit of our communities is the right one, but speaching will keep us from fulfilling that desire [19, 23].

If you know how to listen, you can hear the rumblings that confirm that preaching, as we know it, is a tragically broken endeavor. It can be heard in the halls at every pastors' convention. It can be heard in the conversations among preachers at social gatherings. It can be heard in cars as people drive home from church. You most certainly would be able to hear it if you could crawl into the heads of most preachers during their times of preparation or as they step into the pulpit [6, 10].

It seems clear that we're living in an age containing more great preachers than at any other time in history [4]. We also have greater access to wonderful sermons, and every week in North America more people listen to sermons—live, on the radio or television, on CDs in their cars, and on the Internet—than at any other time in history. But if we look at how Christians continue to struggle with what it means to live in the way of Jesus, we soon realize that great preaching isn't sufficient [11].

Those of us who do the preaching are often the ones who recognize the problem first, not because we think we're bad preachers, but because we know we're good at it [1, 5, 6]. We feel it when our sermons—even those that are technically perfect, those that are relevant and relatable with clever illustrations pulled from popular culture, or those that reveal some deep insight into the text—leave us feeling isolated and ineffectual [19]. We see it when we look at our congregations and see them diligently taking notes we know they'll never look at or watch them nod in agreement with statements they won't remember once brunch is over. We hear it when our parishioners come to us with the same problems and questions we thought we covered so beautifully during that series on the Sermon on the Mount [20].

WHY PREACHING FAILS

I looked through preaching books and talked to many other preachers to find out what they had to say about why preaching doesn't work. They offered four major reasons for the failure of preaching:

The problem is the people. There are those who suggest the reason we aren't seeing the promised effects of preaching (the creation of communities living in harmony with God) is because the people are "hard-hearted" or refuse to listen to the truth. They seem to believe that when the Word of God is preached correctly, it does its part; but if people aren't changed, then it's because they're "the wrong kind of soil" [7].

The problem is the method. Some suggest that we need to add new tricks to our preaching to make our sermons more meaningful to people living in today's culture. They contend that people are different these days and therefore need to have more interactive or experiential communication. We should be using visual reinforcements, fill-in outlines, dramas or well-orchestrated music, and multisensory media experiences to hold the attention and interest of those listening. Some recommend the use of discussion questions for small groups so the broad message can be brought down to a personal level in a more intimate context. In this justification it's the method—not the message—that needs work [7].

The problem is the preacher. If the pastor is the right kind of vessel, some say, then his sermons will work. In other words, if we had better motives or better relationships with God, our preaching would seem fresh, attractive, and powerful [7].

The problem is the content. And finally, there are some who suggest that what we really need is to get to a pure or more authentic message of Jesus, and then we'd see preaching's real power [7].

THE PROBLEM IS SPEACHING

Unfortunately, these reasons fail to tap into the most significant and perhaps most simple reason why speaching doesn't work [1]. The problem is that preaching, as we know it, suffers from a relationship problem. The issue isn't simply how we present the information but whose information it is [15]. The issue isn't simply how we tell the story but the relationship between the teller and the hearers [9, 10]. The issue isn't simply the content we present but where we get that content [21, 22, 34]. The crisis isn't how we preach or what we preach or to whom we preach but the act of preaching itself, which has devolved into speaching [1].

Speaching is not defined by the style of the presentation but by the relationship of the presenter to both the listeners and the content: the pastor uses a lecture-like format, often standing while the listeners are sitting. The speacher decides the content ahead of time, usually in a removed setting, and then offers it in such a way that the speacher is in control of the content, speed, and conclusion of the presentation [31, 32, 33].

Speaching can come in many forms. It can be narrative, didactic, inductive, deductive, or what Len Sweet and Brian McLaren call "abductive" in approach (meaning the sermon seizes people by the imagination and helps them gain a new perspective). Regardless of its form, preaching has so uniformly been equated with speech making that any other means of sermonizing is thought to be trivial and less authoritative. What's worse, speaching is an ineffectual means of communication, one that goes against the very reason we seek to live in Christian community to begin with—so our lives can be shaped as we journey together toward God [24, 26]. My hope is that the conversation in this book will help us free preaching from the limitations of content [8] and move toward a better understanding of the effect of speaching on our communities [11, 25].

I don't think we've allowed preaching to become speaching out of malice or pride, but rather because we've become blind to the ways in which the act of speaching damages our people and creates a sense of powerlessness in them [4, 12]. I don't believe this is what we want. In fact, I believe most of us desperately want to be part of something better, something more. I know I do [6, 25].

As a pastor I want to be part of a community where the workings of God are imbedded in all, where the roles of teaching and learning aren't mine alone but instead are something intrinsic to who we are as a people [19, 22, 23]. The priesthood of all believers was among the greatest contributions of the Reformation and has essentially been ignored in the area of preaching in many of our churches to the point that it could be called "an unfunded mandate of the reformation" [21]. It means we recognize the work of the Spirit of God in the lives of every human being, and God's work can play out in ways that are more meaningful than simply viewing people as a means of fulfilling the church's agenda. This concept can—and must—include God's people *being* the church and leading one another in every area of life together [8, 15, 16].

THE MOVE TO
PROGRESSIONAL DIALOGUE

Speaching stands in contrast to what I call *progressional dialogue*, where the content of the presentation is established in the context of a healthy relationship between the presenter and the listeners, and substantive changes in the content are then created as a result of this relationship.

It works like this: I say something that causes another person to think something she hadn't thought before. In response she says something that causes a third person to make a comment he wouldn't normally have made without the benefit of the second person's statement. In turn *I* think something I wouldn't have thought without hearing the comments made by the other two. So now we've all ended up in a place we couldn't have come to without the input we received from each other [2]. In a real way the conversation has progressed.

This interaction can take place in the very moments in which the comments are made or over time. It may include one of us talking longer than the others or sharing the time more equally. The point is that we are in relationship with one another and we are contributing—through dialogue—to one another's lives [24, 25, 26].

At Solomon's Porch, the church where I'm the pastor, progressional dialogue takes several forms. The two most obvious are the sermon preparation, which involves in-depth conversation with a group of other people from the church [31], and the weekly open discussion that happens during the sermon—I talk for a while and then invite others to share their ideas, input, and thoughts about what's been said [2].

Both speaching and progressional dialogue allow a person to have an opinion or even an agenda. But the progressional dialogue approach doesn't allow us (pastors or parishioners) to stay in one place with our opinions and agendas left unaltered [15, 18]. We're given the opportunity to change, refine, and reframe our ideas about God and our lives as God's people. In other words, we're asked to be the church.

PREACHING: THE SOCIALIZING
FORCE OF COMMUNITY

Preaching isn't simply something a pastor does; it's a socializing force and a formative practice in a community [9, 10]. The way we approach preaching is among the most important considerations for those who are seeking to live with God in new ways. Preaching has a tremendous history in the church [4]. It may be said there would be no Christianity without preaching. Churches typically include some sort of preaching in their collective gatherings, and there are many traditions that use preaching more frequently and with more emphasis than communion, collective prayer, personal testimony, healing touch, or other spiritual practices. In fact, for many, church doesn't really count unless it includes a time of preaching [13].

Because of the power and importance of preaching, it's crucial that the church, if it seeks to be useful in the world, be attentive to the effects of speaching and do whatever is necessary to protect our communities from the significant problems speaching presents.

Please understand I'm not suggesting that speaching is a poison that cannot be consumed in even the smallest amounts [7]. There are times when a community will be well-served by the speaching act. But the cumulative effect is another story; consider that it isn't an occasional practice that provides formation, either for good or ill, but one that is replicated time and time again. Weekly speaching functions like a repetitive stress disorder for both preacher and parish [9, 10, 15, 18, 19]. Occasional usage likely won't hurt anyone, but to make a regular practice of speaching may well be an act of relational violence, one that is detrimental to the very communities we are seeking to nurture [22, 23].

I can imagine a church—and a people—who see themselves as preachers in one another's lives. Not preachers with inarguable speeches, but people who engage, inform, and build life into one another. Any preaching practice that results in less collective interaction and building of one another should be used very sparingly and abandoned as soon as possible [25, 39].

This is my hope for what preaching can be: the mutual admonition of one another in life with God. The plain reality is that speaching is not adequate to accomplish this. Preaching is far too valuable to be reduced to speech making. I'm not suggesting we become a people who spend less time telling the story, less time talking, or less time leading one another, but certainly less time using one-way communication as our primary means of talking about and thinking about the gospel [19]. I'm not suggesting a practice that reduces speaking, but one that encourages more. What I'm advocating is that we become communities who listen to the preachers among us, not just the preacher standing in front of us [21, 22].

A HISTORY OF SPEACHING

I've been a pastor long enough to have attended many pastors' events. At nearly every one of them at least some time has been devoted to conversations about preaching. In recent years I've been struck by how readily speaching has been accepted as the biblical form of preaching [4]. This saddens me. Preaching has a rich and important history with more usefulness, beauty, commonality, and truthfulness than speaching allows. Preaching means "proclaiming." It doesn't mean inarguable, one-way communication. Look at the places in the Bible where preaching is mentioned, such as this passage from Romans: "For, 'Everyone who calls on the name of the Lord will be saved.' How, then, can they call on the one they have not believed in? And how can they believe in the one of whom they have not heard? And how can they hear without someone preaching to them?" (Romans 10:13-14). It's inconceivable to insert the words "giving a speech" in place of the depth and transformative power of preaching.

Despite our insistence on speaching, churches know there is often too much influence in this practice of one-way communication, so they attempt to push people into small groups to compensate for it. Still we continue to stand in front of our congregations and offer them our well-crafted speeches, hoping that somehow they'll find meaning in our words [12, 13, 14].

We find ourselves stuck, then, with a way of preaching that doesn't work but without any sense of how to change it. It's ironic to me that those who advocate a more holistic means of communication and spiritual formation have to justify why they want something more than speaching. It's the speaching act that has some explaining to do. It's as if speaching is the orthodox way, and the more communal approach suggested by progressional dialogue is the new kid on the block who has to prove herself. In reality speaching is quite new, a creation of Enlightenment Christianity in which faith formation was understood as something best handled by the "expert" (aka the pastor) [4, 15, 19].

Perhaps one of the reasons we have a hard time letting go of speaching is that people seem to like it [12]. Good speaching brings good feedback. But the value of speaching is not determined by the number of people who say they appreciate it; there may be more people now than ever before who prefer to sit as passive recipients and trust the expert to tell them what the Bible says and what and how they should think. At a time when we are the most speached-to church in history, our understanding of Christianity has become increasingly fractured and self-absorbed. And to be honest, if numbers were truly the mark by which we judged the success of a church, we'd have little choice but to look at the statistics that say the church population in North America is not increasing at nearly the same rate as the general population and therefore conclude that speaching is indeed failing as a means of "winning souls for Christ." The value of our practices—including preaching—ought to be judged by their effects on our communities and the ways in which they help us move toward life with God [11, 25].

So far I've come up with five specific effects that speaching has on communities of faith (there are undoubtedly more). You might be surprised to discover that the effects on this list may not, on the surface, appear to be problems. Rather we might be inclined to see them as good things—even benefits to our communities. Some might even find that this list represents exactly what they've been hoping their preaching will do; our understanding of preaching is the outgrowth of our assumptions about—among other things—God, people, the world, time, and the church. Certainly there are ways of understanding God, faith, and humanity in which these effects of speaching are quite desirable. But to my mind these effects are detrimental to the kinds of communities I believe we're all seeking to nurture.

CREATES ONE SEAT OF GODLY AUTHORITY

Speaching sets the story of God in a prefabricated context where it all makes sense from the perspective of the person speaking. The context of others is therefore inconsequential. Speaching also creates a belief that even in the presence of dozens, hundreds, even thousands of other Christians, there are a select few who know God's truth and who get to tell others about God. There is hardly a preacher who wants her hearers to leave with the notion that they must access the truth of God through the preacher. But that is precisely the message speaching perpetuates: The pastor has the authority to speak about God, and you don't. When communities are convinced they are better off with a unified understanding of God that is best articulated by trained presenters, we end up with people who cannot translate what they hear in church to the way they live their lives [17, 18, 19].

PROVIDES ONE CLEAR MESSAGE

The message at the heart of Christianity is that there is good news among us, that God is among us, that God has not abandoned us. This good news lives not only in the Bible stories, but also in the lives of people. The gospel expands as it moves out into the world through God's people. When we limit the message to one person's speaching act, we may gain clarity, but we close ourselves off to the ways in which the gospel can seep into the corners of individual lives. The message of the speaker will always be generalized, never specific. It will always be presented from the same understanding of the world, the same set of experiences, and the same framework for what it means to live in the kingdom. The goal of preaching is to build one another with the abundance of good news and the continuous, contagious story of the expanding message of God. When we have a centralized message, we eliminate a terrific amount of understanding about the life of God. When we move away from speaching and give voice to the myriad ways in which the gospel infiltrates the lives of all people, we unleash the depth of life with God and allow it to mean something to us as individuals, not simply as congregations [15, 16, 17].

OFFERS A SENSE OF CONTROL

It seems to make sense that one of the pastor's jobs is to take the huge, complex mass that is the gospel and funnel it into something more easily handled by the untrained individual. But the story we tell is one of God moving in ways we cannot control or even understand. We are telling the story of God creating and inviting us to create, of God moving in the life of people all around the world, the story of God using the unlikely—the old, the virginal, the meek, the crucified. We tell the story of God inviting us all into the story. We tell the story of raging seas calmed and raging love lived. We tell the story of the Spirit blowing where it will. Yet we resort to speaching in an effort to protect the story, to make it digestible and applicable. The gospel is simply too powerful for that kind of control [18].

REINFORCES A PARTICULAR KIND OF RELATIONSHIP WITH THE BIBLE

Speaching places the story of God in the hands of the presenter in such a way that it creates distance between the hearers and the source of the story. Speaching has a way of making the Bible fit into the presentation. It often becomes the content that supports our presuppositions, rather than being a participant in a conversation. The Bible is more than a source of our faith. The Bible ought to live as an authoritative member of our community, one to whom we listen on all topics of which she speaks. Speaching takes the Bible away from the hearers—many of whom are already intimidated by the Bible—and reminds them they are not in a position to speak on how they are implicated by this story. Instead their relationship with the story of God and God's work in the lives of God's people—a story they are part of, mind you—is controlled by the speacher's choice of text and message [32, 33, 34].

REINFORCES A PARTICULAR
KIND OF RELATIONSHIP BETWEEN
PASTOR AND CONGREGATION

I crave connection with the people in my community, not because I'm the pastor but because, like all of us, I am meant to live in relationship with others. When the pastor is seen as one whose relationship with the story is to be the teller instead of a community member who shares in the formation of the story, we put the preacher in an unsustainable place of pressure and isolation. There is something dangerous in the life of the preacher who regularly tells others how things are, could be, or ought to be.

Speaching also strips away any chance for people in the congregation to feel known and understood by their pastor. Great speech makers have tricks they use to connect with their audience—picking a couple of people and looking at them during their speech, using examples from the hometown crowd to build a sense of intimacy, that sort of thing. But these are manipulations, not relationships [6]. Like the presidential candidate who uses the story of poor Martha Lewis and her arthritis to help him make a point about insurance costs, the speacher who is disconnected from her hearers risks turning God's children into little more than sermon illustrations [9, 10].

Even those of us who might be aware of the damaging impact of speaching have had a hard time replacing it with something else. As I've looked over my own experiences as a pastor and speacher, I've come to believe there are several reasons why we continue to use speaching as a legitimate form of communication in our communities [12].

Our communities demand it. We know people like to hear us speach, particularly if we're good at it. We believe that if we stop doing it, then they'll stop coming. And that might be true; there are growing numbers of people who not only prefer preaching as speaching, but they also require it. Many people come to church because they want to have a person in their lives who makes Christianity accessible and understandable. The preacher in the speaching act can often do exactly that [8].

But many of us who have seen significant growth in our churches know a dirty little secret: Significant growth has its own ill effect on helping communities develop deep faith. Numeric growth of Christianity doesn't indicate a more harmonious way of life with God. The metaphor of the body is a good one for churches. A body that's too big puts a strain on the systems of the body. At the same time communities who never embrace new people or new perspectives find themselves starving. Both obesity and starvation are pathways to death.

We have few options. Even when we do feel a need for change, the way to make that change happen can be hard to figure out. Many of us have the impulse to try something new—sometimes out of desperation, sometimes out of hopeful experimentation—but time and creative energy are the enemies of innovation. When there are dozens, hundreds, even thousands of people waiting in a room to hear the speech each week, it's daunting to think of doing something different or unexpected. Because the instinct to make a change is not supported, there is great risk in moving beyond the "tried and true" practices into new territory. Who wants to be the one to derail a church by trying some weird new preaching idea [14]?

We like the kinds of communities that like speachers. There are many professional and personal benefits to being in communities with high regard for speachers. We are treated well, and we get a strong sense of job security. The role of the pastor and the prestige that comes with it have changed significantly in the last 150 years, leaving few benefits. But if we give good speeches, we earn back that lost prestige. We may get speaking gigs, book deals, TV appearances. Speaching is perhaps the only part of a pastor's job where we get feedback, where we find some standard against which to measure our "success." It can be tremendously difficult to put that kind of acceptance in jeopardy [23].

There is no call to re-imagine it. When we don't believe we are called or even given permission to change, we rarely make change happen. There is plenty of support for reconsidering other aspects of church life: worship styles, organization, denominationalism, and so on. But few are calling for a change in speaching. There are many who don't see how providing new ways of being in the world are part of a pastor's role. Instead they focus on providing new tools to better accomplish the conventional ways of being the church. They fine-tune what was created for another time and place but never think about re-creating it altogether [26].

These reasons may have held us back from exploring new ways of preaching, but they're no match for a pastor who is passionate about finding a better way to help the faith community live out its call to live as the people of God. This call to a new way of preaching is a call to being a new people, a new church. Part of becoming this new people is developing a deep ecclesiology.

DEEP ECCLESIOLOGY

Through the centuries followers of Jesus have sought to live in harmony with God, one another, and their world. This effort has involved the creation of Christian communities who articulate, express, and embody the hopeful message of God in their lives. Preaching is meant to contribute to this. I'm not suggesting we need a new kind of preaching to reach a target market. Rather we need a new kind of preaching because we need a new us. It's simply not legitimate to continue with the same practices but expect new outcomes. New outcomes are precisely what we need if the church is going to remain prophetic in the lives of God's people [24, 25, 26].

This call for a deep ecclesiology is a cry from the inside. There might very well be benefit to those on the outside who are interested in learning more about living lives of faith, but the move away from speaching is essential for those of us who are already on the inside of these communities and who long to become a new people.

IMPLICATION OVER APPLICATION

One of the greatest areas of change for communities of faith who make an adjustment from the speaching model to the progressional dialogue approach is in our understanding of the role of the story in our lives. As speachers we've become proficient at making every speech applicable to the widest cross-section of people [8]. We've become very good at telling people how this story applies to the lives of strangers [9]. But the very nature of speaching—one person choosing, researching, and preparing the content of the speech—makes it impossible for our speeches to apply to anyone in concrete, meaningful ways. It's an isolated act with an isolated effect.

Because we've been wed to speaching for so long, we've trained our communities to respond to our speeches by asking themselves, *How does this apply to me?* as though the Word of God is some topical ointment. More often than not they will come up with some generic application—be nice to my neighbors, be honest in my relationships, and so on. But is that really the best we can offer our communities?

A better response, one that comes out of a progressional approach to preaching, is one that invites those who take part in the sermon to ask, "If this is our story, what will this mean for our lives?" Consider what would happen if the people in our communities felt *implicated* by the story of God, if our preaching became the impetus for them to become part of the story itself and start arranging their lives around it [11].

One night my wife, Shelley, and I were driving on a major highway in Minneapolis. There is a digital sign positioned on one of the overpasses that allows the traffic department to make road announcements. On the evening we were driving the sign was lit with this message: AMBER ALERT: CHILD ABDUCTION. GREY CHEVROLET BLAZER LICENSE JAB 934. Without a word Shelley and I instantly started looking at all the vehicles around us. This was not our child who was abducted. We knew, or at least assumed, our children were safe. But we were drawn into the story and instinctively knew we had a part to play in it.

Our response to seeing the Amber Alert was different than it would have been had we simply read about the abduction in the paper. We were not spectators of the story but participants who were being asked to do something with this information. We were not asking how this alert applied to our children or to the safety of children in general. This was a call for us and for everyone else driving on that highway to do what we could to remedy the situation. While the chances were remote that we would see the wanted vehicle, we were implicated in this event nonetheless. It became *our* event, if even for a brief time.

We've all been in situations where we suddenly understood that our lives had just changed forever. You find out you're having a baby, you lose your job, the police show up at your house with your 16-year-old in tow. When these situations arise, we don't ask, "How does this apply to me?" We understand that this new chapter in our story will require something of us—a change in our assumptions, our actions, our priorities. The question of implication is not one made by a removed, objective decision maker but by a participant in the story. Our role is to locate ourselves in the story of God, not simply to see how other people's experiences apply to our lives.

Implicatory preaching cannot happen when our speeches are created in isolation [31]. It cannot come from one person's perspective delivered in the broadest generic terms for a mass of passive strangers whose only role is to listen and try to apply thoughts that may or may not have any bearing on their lives [8, 9]. It takes an incarnated story, one that finds its place in the reality of our lives, to reach implication. Implication is more than poignant application. Application is born in the speaker who predetermines the main points with hopes of specific application. Implication is birthed in the dance between the story and the lives of the participants in that story.

This isn't an effort to create hip churches with a novel way of telling the same story. I'm suggesting we need a new story—not just new content but new ideas about the way the story is lived [7, 11, 25]. This story will require new practices so we can better live out the profound implications of the gospel.

THE PRACTICES OF PROGRESSIONAL DIALOGUE

Over the years churches have developed particular skills that allow speaching to continue. Very few of these skills come naturally; they are acquired over time and through steady usage. Progressional dialogue will require our communities—preachers and congregations alike—to develop new ways of being the church [27].

RE-IMAGINED PREPARATION

One of the significant differences between progressional dialogue preaching and speaching is how we create the sermon; the way something is prepared changes its function [30]. If the function of preaching is mutual edification, then the creation of the preaching must be a collective act [31]. Each person and community will need to forge its own path of collective preparation, but it seems to me the following elements need be present in some amount: dialogue, immersion in the story (the Bible, the world, and people's lives) [34], listening, experimentation, disagreement (among each other and within oneself) [29], and openness to others [28, 40].

DELIVERY

The way communities interact with the sermon is as important as the content itself. Sociologists recognize how culture (the shaping and reinforcing pressure on people) includes thoughts (mental categories), desires (what we want to be), intuitions (assumptions for how things are), and tools (the means of supporting life). These ingredients have a symbiotic relationship: The way we live informs what can be desired.

Our intuitions allow us to think about certain things. The tools we use allow certain desires, beliefs, and longings.

In churches we create the boundaries of what will be accepted in this cultural context. The ways in which we allow and access the thoughts, desires, and intuitions of the community will influence the tools we're able to access. So it matters who speaks and how their words are delivered.

The use of provisional statements ("It seems to me...," "As I understand it...," and so on) is an essential aspect of creating a culture of openness and invitation. These words make room for the thoughts and experiences of others [35, 36, 37, 38].

In addition, it's useful to quote others from the community (these quotes often come out of the communal preparation process). Many of us quote experts or famous people who are rarely part of our community. But the people who are in the midst of our communities often have as much to say about how we pursue the life of God as do famous and brilliant strangers [21].

LISTENING

For nearly all trained preachers the skill of listening to the congregation is secondary to listening to the text and interpreting it [39]. Just as medical schools have gone to great lengths in recent years to be sure their students know not only medicine and anatomy but also how to engage in the lives of their patients, so does the pastoral field need to expand to include the skills needed to understand the contexts in which people hear and experience the things of God.

In the last few years preachers have been trained to use mass communication strategies in an effort to increase the impact of their preaching [38]. However, I suggest we instead look at interpersonal communication skills as a means of inviting our congregations into more meaningful lives with God [20].

ASSUMPTIONS OF PROGRESSIONAL DIALOGUE

To be fair the idea that progressional preaching can implicate us in such a way that we move into a deeper life with God is itself based on several assumptions. Just as the assumptions about speaching inform the reasons we stick with it in spite of the evidence of its failure, so too do these assumptions about progressional preaching suggest something about the kinds of communities in which we see ourselves living [2].

ASSUMES GOD'S TRUTH RESIDES IN ALL PEOPLE

The only way progressional preaching makes sense is if we believe the people we are progressing with have something to add [22, 40]. While no pastor I know would suggest that he and he alone holds the key to God's truth, few churches live out the idea of the "priesthood of all believers" in this tangible way [17, 21]. Not only is it a theological imperative to allow the Spirit of God to live and find a voice in all members of our communities, but it's also increasingly a sociological necessity as well. As our churches become more reflective of our multicultural society, we simply cannot pretend to speak to the enormous array of histories, perspectives, and experiences represented by the people who make up our communities of faith [40]. Progressional preaching is perhaps the only way to access the truth that resides in the hearts of our brothers and sisters [15].

The story told about the early church in the book of Acts hinges on the story of Peter and Cornelius in chapter 10. Up to this point the church was still struggling with the "Gentile question." After this encounter with a faith-filled Gentile, all the major players—even Peter—were changed, and the story becomes active with the faith of the Gentiles. We witness the shift in Peter's perspective when he finishes the story for Cornelius. When Peter says in verse 34, "I now realize how true it is that God does not show favoritism," this isn't an incidental comment. It's the result of progressional preaching where the preacher and the hearer are both made more aware of the life of God through dialogue with one another [3].

PROVIDES A FULLER UNDERSTANDING
OF THE STORY

The call to be a people who live in the entire story of God's work in the world is a call to be engaged with the story in ways that speaching doesn't allow [21, 22]. When we speach, we provide one view, one understanding, one piece of the story [5, 15, 16, 18]. When we hear from others, we aren't inviting competing notions set in opposition to one another, but new insights into the story that implicates us all [11]. Not only does this allow the hearers to find multiple entry points into the story, but it also validates the work God is doing in the lives of those who speak. Suddenly, their experiences do matter.

There are those who assume that if more people are allowed to share their understanding of teaching, theology, and faith, then there's a greater risk of the church losing truth [16, 17]. But the history of heresy shows it's most often the abuse of power—not an openness of power—that creates environments ripe with heresy. The church is at a greater risk of losing its message when we limit those who can tell the story versus when we invite the community to know and refine it [18].

SHIFTS CONTROL TO GOD

The activity of God is clearly beyond our comprehension and control. Yet when we create neat, three-point packages to explain away the mysteries of God's work and leave no room for our hearers to ask their questions or express their thoughts, we send a clear message that God can be mastered. Progressional preaching assumes there will always be more to say than one person can say alone [28, 31]. There will always be questions and wonderings and puzzlement over the ways of God. It assumes we cannot work out the questions of faith on our own but need to be in communities of faith in which we journey together toward a deeper understanding of God. It assumes no one person can master all knowledge or understanding, and we gain so much when we interact with the lives and thoughts of others. Most importantly, it assumes that *God* sets the agenda, not us [15, 19, 23].

ALTERS THE COMMUNITY'S
RELATIONSHIP WITH THE BIBLE

The contemporary church makes two mistakes regarding the function and relationship of the Bible. One is to think of her as a stagnant telling of all the desires of God. The other is to think of her as something from which we extract truth, whether in the form of moral teaching or propositional statements [32, 33, 34].

Progressional dialogue creates a relationship in which the Bible becomes a living member of the community [34]. I've found that when others are allowed to speak, they often refer to parts of the Bible that are seemingly unrelated to the passage on which the sermon is based. But I am constantly amazed at how their insights or sense of a passage add depth to what I've said or spark ideas from others in our community. When this happens, the Bible becomes part of our conversation, not a dead book from which I extract truth.

ALTERS THE RELATIONSHIP BETWEEN
PASTOR AND CONGREGATION

I find tremendous freedom in knowing I don't carry the weight of all knowledge and application in my preaching [19]. The communal act of dialogue allows me to be fully me and lets my understanding shine with the confidence that others may correct what I miss or misconstrue. It allows me to be a part of my community because I am no longer in a position of having to be the answer man. I am now a brother—granted, one who talks a lot—who is taking part in the life of a community. I can be vulnerable about my own questions and wonderings, knowing my community doesn't expect me to be the sole purveyor of truth and wisdom [16]. This seems to me to be a much more sustainable relationship with my church than one in which I'm always the expert who can't let my guard down.

Progressional dialogue has also allowed me access into the lives of the people in my community. I can almost predict who will comment after my sermons because I know their issues and concerns [10]. They trust I know the context of their comments and can therefore allow themselves to be more open, more honest, and more vulnerable as they take part in the dialogue. We often leave our gatherings not asking, "How does this apply to me?" but openly working out the implications of the story in which we are playing roles.

The message of Jesus is that the truth of God is within us and not limited to the temple or to any other holy place. Jesus often pointed to the life of God within the outsider, the reviled, the ordinary. The notion that God can only be accessed through the well-trained, special, called-out person sits in contrast to the very gospel of Jesus [21, 22]. The prophetic call of the good news is that God is alive and well in the lives of all God's people.

Progressional preaching has a dangerous quality to it [11, 40]. What kind of faith will we have if the preselected, educated ones are not setting the agenda? What kind of faith will we have if our content is not prescreened and "genericized" to meet the masses? What kind of faith will we have if regular people are putting their spin on it? What kind of faith will we have if we ask what the story has in mind for us? What kind of faith will we have if we listen to the outsider *and* the insider?

What kind of faith will we have? Maybe a dangerous faith. Maybe a Christian faith. Maybe a faith worth preaching.

SECTION THREE
A MOVE TO SOMETHING NEW

CHAPTER 1

SPEACHING VS. PREACHING

Throughout this book, I will use the term *speaching* to discuss the ways in which preaching has degraded into speech making. I use this word to distinguish speaching, which I believe to be a form of speaking that is inconsistent with the outcomes we want to see arise from our preaching, from the act of preaching, which I believe to be a good, right, and essential calling of the church.

When you think about it, preaching is a cultural oddity. It's a strange mix of public speaking and intimate soul care. Because we believe preaching to be one of the ways in which we minister to our congregations, nearly every preacher would rightly cringe at the notion that preaching is just giving a speech or a lecture. Yet most preaching is done in such a way that it's hard to understand it as anything *other* than a speech that happens to have religious content. The "speacher" stands in front of the "audience." The speaker is the only one with a microphone and therefore the only one with the power to speak on the subject at hand. The content of the speech has been decided on with little, if any, input from those who are hearing the speech, and the conclusions drawn are those drawn by the speaker and no one else.

My contention is that this way of preaching hurts our communities. Because speaching is reinforced with religious significance, it sends the message to the hearers that not only are they invited to draw the same conclusions but that they also ought to out of religious conviction. For many the thought of disagreeing with a sermon is tantamount to disbelief. That is what makes speaching particularly insidious. There are few places in our culture where ideas are communicated from positions of power to audiences who have no way to contribute to the content: political speeches, music concerts, television infomercials, and convention plenary sessions come to mind. Yet political speeches are uniformly met with counterarguments; even the President's State of the Union address is followed by a rebuttal from the other party. While a musician in a concert can give unchecked expression to her opinions for a night, the listeners always have the ability to stop buying the CDs and concert tickets that sustain her career. Infomercials are regularly turned off by the very people they are meant to engage. And it's never a problem to walk out on a convention speech.

In a church setting, however, these tools of response or rejection are rarely provided for the listener. It's ironic to me that in forums where people are dealing with the most ordinary questions of life, they are given ample opportunity for input. But in church, where people are dealing with the very core of their existence, we offer them no such opportunity.

Dustin is part of our church, and he works in the advertising industry. Not long ago he and I had a conversation about the ethical issues involved in advertising. He described what are, in his opinion, the two ethical intentions of marketing and advertising. He said that contrary to people's perceptions, marketers aren't seeking to convince people to buy things they don't want; that would involve manipulation and dishonesty. What they're doing instead is providing more options and building product loyalty.

He used two examples. The first was pizza. Advertisers aren't trying to make the people who don't want pizza eat a large supreme with extra cheese. On the contrary, they're just saying, "If you like Domino's pizza, you should try Papa John's." The other means of building product loyalty is clearly seen in car advertising. Dustin said, "When you see a Jetta commercial, you might conclude, 'I would never buy that car just from seeing that commercial,' but that's not the point. We're trying to help those who have already bought a Jetta feel they have made a good choice so they will be more likely to do it again."

In some ways speaching is like this form of marketing. People want to go to a church where they can hear a clear message that reassures them they made a good choice, that their theology is the right one. They go not to be disturbed and formed but to be comforted. Despite the prevalence of speaching, I don't really believe most pastors are willing to settle for offering their congregations comfort in place of life-changing spiritual formation.

As you read these thoughts, perhaps you feel I'm suggesting little more than a new *method* of preaching. But to me there is no way to separate the method from the message. As I will argue throughout the book, the way we "speech" creates a certain understanding of God, faith, life, authority, and power that is detrimental to the message we are attempting to live and communicate as pastors.

CHAPTER 2

UNDERSTANDING PROGRESSIONAL DIALOGUE

For the purposes of this conversation I am saying a "speach" is a well-crafted statement with points that build upon one another. It might be narrative, propositional, inductive, or deductive. The speacher has decided ahead of time where the message is going and has carefully crafted the speech to ensure that the hearers receive that message.

Progressional dialogue, on the other hand, involves the intentional interplay of multiple viewpoints that leads to unexpected and unforeseen ideas. The message will change depending on who is present and who says what. This kind of preaching is dynamic in the sense that the outcome is determined on the spot by the participants.

Consider that Paul's epistles are all part of an ongoing dialogue with those who are on the receiving end of these letters. Paul writes to various communities with answers to questions they've had, advice for dealing with situations particular to those communities, even admonishments for behaviors that trouble him. The letters typically end with Paul telling the readers he will see them soon so they can continue this progressional dialogue.

In Matthew 13 there is an interesting account of Jesus returning to his hometown where he is met with criticism and disrespect. The last part of the passage reads, "He did not do many miracles there because of their lack of faith" (vs. 58). It seems the miracles of Jesus are dynamic—influenced by who is present and the context of the situation. Is it really that big a stretch to believe that our sermons can be influenced by the same factors?

When I've talked with other pastors about progressional preaching, their concerns are nearly always about heresy. They're concerned that if they open the floor to anyone who feels like speaking, they will lose control over the message, and all hell—literally—will break loose. I understand this concern. As pastors we spend years in theological training to make sure we know what we're talking about and that we're informed, educated leaders who won't toss out crazy ideas about God to the masses. We often belong to denominations that take great pains to set out their ideas about orthodoxy and correct doctrine. We study our commentaries before every sermon to check and double-check our thoughts against the wisdom of the experts. If we go through all of this, certainly we can't trust just anyone to offer relevant insight into something as precious as the Word of God.

But I've found this concern to be unfounded in the practice of progressional dialogue. Far from pulling us in the direction of heresy, including collective conversation in our sermon time has in many, many instances led to greater understanding for the people in our community. In fact, I find that working out our questions and wonderings in the context of the group actually prevents the heretical thinking so easily found in individuated expressions of faith. When people set their ideas on the table, those who might lean toward heresy or idiocy are quickly called out by the group.

One night at our church a man said some things during the discussion time that were extremely hurtful to some members of our community. Fighting every urge I had to defend our community, I sat and waited to see what would happen. While several people spoke of experiences that directly refuted the things this man said about our church, no one was argumentative or mean-spirited. By the end of a very emotional exchange we hadn't made any new decisions or settled a conflict of ideology. Instead we found ourselves having to listen to one another and to wrestle with the reality that we come to our community with differences that need to be taken seriously if we truly are to be the body of Christ.

Progressional dialogue doesn't mean groupthink, discussion, or even agreement. It means we listen to one another in such a way that what we think cannot be left unchanged. We hear what others in our community are saying and have no choice but to let it impact our thinking. Progressional dialogue means moving forward into new thoughts, not digging into predetermined positions. It means being open to—even expecting—change, just as those we're in conversation with are changed.

CHAPTER 3

PETER AND CORNELIUS

There is an exceptionally clear picture of the life-altering power of progressional dialogue in the book of Acts: the story of Peter and Cornelius. I would go so far as to say this story marks a turning point for the early church, one that wouldn't have happened if Peter had been unwilling to move beyond speech making as his primary means of communicating the gospel.

In its earliest incarnation the church was living out a synagogue mentality. The people of Jesus' day understood him as being the prophet of the God of Israel. So there was significant backing for the perspective that Jesus' story was a reclaiming of the Jewish story in which Gentiles would need to enter through the Jewish door. This led to many questions and conflicts for the early Christians. The second chapter of Galatians gives a bit of insight into the intensity of the struggle over the question of Gentile participation in the gospel of Jesus.

But in the book of Acts the early church leaders began to understand that God's intention is for *all* of creation to come to fullness in God, each in its own setting. In other words, conversion to Judaism was not a prerequisite for Christian faith.

For years in the life of the early church, Peter resisted offering his complete support of the notion that Christianity should move outside the bounds of Judaism. His background is important to remember as we read the story of his meeting with Cornelius (told in Acts 10 and again in Acts 11). The story begins with Cornelius, who is described as a God-fearing man or one who has the attention of God. Later in the story it becomes clear that Cornelius wasn't yet baptized by the Holy Spirit. While he may have had some familiarity with the happenings of Jesus, it's safe to say he had nothing resembling the common faith of that day.

In a vision an angel told Cornelius that he ought to send his men to Joppa and bring back a man named Peter who could be found staying in a house by the sea. Cornelius did just as the angel told him.

Meanwhile, Peter, in keeping with his prayer and meditation practices, was in the midst of one of his thrice-daily prayer experiences when he had a vision as well. Peter's vision was more cryptic. It involved a sheet with animals on it—animals that Peter had always understood to be unclean (the same categorization Peter used for the Gentiles). In the vision God told Peter to eat these animals, but Peter refused on the grounds that he had never and would never defile himself in such a way. I find this an interesting interaction. Peter claimed to take the moral and religious "high ground." But we can see that if he had maintained his conviction, he would have missed out greatly on what God was up to.

As Peter's vision continued, the sheet was taken away and Peter was startled from his meditative state by the men sent by Cornelius the day before. The men explained their reason for being there and Peter invited them to stay the night before he joined them on their return journey to Caesarea. The story doesn't tell us what happened that evening or what they talked about, but I assume somewhere along the line Peter connected his vision's call to eat unclean food with Cornelius's vision to send for him. It must have been a mind bender for Peter to consider that God was somehow inviting him into some kind of life with this unclean Gentile.

The next morning Peter accompanied the men. After traveling for a few days, they arrived at Cornelius's home, which was full of people who were excited and expectant to hear what Peter would say. It's not clear if Cornelius knew about Peter's vision and how these two different men were connected; but when Peter entered the house, Cornelius greeted him by bowing at his feet. Cornelius was obviously impressed with this man the angel had named in his vision. Peter told him that despite the laws prohibiting Jews from meeting with Gentiles, God had made it clear to Peter that he had other plans. Peter then said, "May I ask why you sent for me?" (Acts 10:29) This is a wonderful posture of progressional dialogue, one that acknowledges that the other person has an agenda as well.

Cornelius then explained his part of the story, to which Peter responded:

I now realize how true it is that God does not show favoritism but accepts those from every nation who fear him and do what is right. You know the message God sent to the people of Israel, announcing the good news of peace through Jesus Christ, who is Lord of all. You know what has happened throughout the province of Judea, beginning in Galilee after the baptism that John preached—how God anointed Jesus of Nazareth with the Holy Spirit and power, and how he went around doing good and healing all who were under the power of the devil, because God was with him. We are witnesses of everything he did in the country of the Jews and in Jerusalem. They killed him by hanging him on a cross, but God raised him from the dead on the third day and caused him to be seen. He was not seen by all the people, but by witnesses whom God had already chosen—by us who ate and drank with him after he rose from the dead. He commanded us to preach to the people and to testify that he is the one whom God appointed as judge of the living and the dead. All the prophets testify about him that everyone who believes in him receives forgiveness of sins through his name. (Acts 10:34-43)

Peter declares that these Gentiles are part of the same story and commands they be baptized into the community of faith; I'm not sure we can fully grasp the depth of change this must have been for Peter. He was the "rock," the great apostle. Yet even after years of ministry, even after all the preaching he'd done, he needed to change yet again to remain true to the things of God. I don't think it's an overstatement to say Peter was forced to rethink all he had done to this point. Are we above such a call to be willing to rethink what we believe to be right and true when we're faced with the greater truth of God?

Acts 11 goes on to record how the leaders in Jerusalem had real problems with the rumor that Peter had entered the house of a Gentile and had eaten with the people there. So Peter recounted to them the story of his vision and Cornelius's vision, and the leaders in Jerusalem were said to be in agreement that God had granted life to the Gentiles.

I think it's safe to say that this acceptance of the Gentiles by the Jewish church was among the most important events of the New Testament era. And it took place through a preaching interaction that included intertwined stories and the activity of God ahead of the obedient actions of people (even the most unlikely people) and resulted in the conversion of not only the recipient, but also the preacher.

If only this could be the norm for our preaching today.

CHAPTER 4

THE ROOTS OF SPEACHING

To those of us who are schooled in the modern Christian tradition, anything that moves us away from our trusted sermons feels like a break from the accepted standards of good preaching. In reality preaching as speaching is quite new. In fact, it is the creation of Enlightenment Christianity.

Not long ago I had a conversation with Peter Drucker, a well-known cultural commentator and business guru. He said, "There are few factors that have shaped American society as much as the rise of the contemporary megachurch." He is not using the term *megachurch* to refer only to our current versions in the ever-expanding suburbs, but rather to the large, dominant church that has been part of nearly every American city since the beginning of the twentieth century. It's the form of church that was produced in the wake of the industrial revolution as people moved from rural communities and parish churches to urban communities and urban churches.

In cities and rural areas the role of the pastor, the role of the parishioner, and the very nature of the church experience changed dramatically in the late nineteenth and early twentieth centuries. In her book *When Church Became Theatre: The Transformation of Evangelical Architecture and*

Worship in Nineteenth-Century America, Jeanne Halgren Kilde does a wonderful job of describing the social dynamics that caused the church to shift from the cathedral and meeting house models to the stage-focused systems still being used today. She explains how the theater became so powerful in western culture that many churches began to utilize it as a metaphor and built their buildings to allow for it. While this change in metaphor had great impact on church architecture in the late 1800s, Kilde explains it had an even greater impact on the role of the pastor. The position of pastor changed from being a member of the community with a unique connection with God—a change I heartily applaud—to being the main player on the stage with the congregation as the audience (and that's the end of the applause). This new metaphor changed the pastor's relationship with the congregation in myriad ways, not the least of which was in the area of preaching. Over time the issue in the minds of the pastor and parishioner was not *How are we living with God?* but *What do you have for me to hear?*

As the population shifted to the cities, rural communities could no longer support their own residential pastors, giving rise to the itinerant preacher. The people in these communities went from having a small church filled with people—including a pastor—they saw every day to meeting in large tents set up in some random location meant to attract the largest number of people from any given area. People found themselves sitting in huge temporary rooms with Christians from varied backgrounds. Then a speaker would take the stage, someone who didn't know the people but knew the Bible and could talk about it in effortless tones for what seemed like endless sessions. This experience of hearing a stranger speak about the Bible in ways that made sense to people's lives began to shape not only the people who were attracted or converted, but also the preachers in the remaining local congregations. Imagine the pressure the local pastor felt to use this same approach to help his congregation understand the Bible.

This same era also saw the birth of Sunday school, not only as a means of religious instruction but also as an extra day of school for poor children. It became a way of bringing new people into the church, people who needed to be educated in the Christian life. The use of speaching to evangelize these disparate constituencies was not only effective, but it was also novel. People were experiencing this kind of church for the first time, and they loved it.

Preaching as speaching clearly had a usefulness in that time and place. But some 100 years later it seems we ought to be willing to take the same kinds of risks that these Christians did and create novel ways of communicating with people who live in a new and challenging time. But I find that trying to free preaching from the speech making act is something like mothers in the 1970s explaining why they wanted to return to breast-feeding after decades of professional advice promoted the use of synthetic formula. It's difficult to justify the more natural expression when the synthetic has become the norm.

One of the ways we preach to one another in our community is to create ways of assisting each other with real-life issues. An example of this is when my wife was leading a "life development forum" on natural health living. Shelley, like many in our community, is thoughtful about how we relate to one another. She was talking to me about what the next steps could be for her group, which had just finished its three consecutive meetings. She said, "The problem is, not to brag or anything, but I could talk about this stuff all day long. I know a lot about it. I'm just not sure if it helps for me to keep talking about all I know. It seems like we're now to the point where we need to start dealing with each person's particular situation."

Shelley's impulse is one felt by many of us pastors who are seeking to move toward a more progressional approach. We do know a lot. We know more than most people in our communities about the stuff we talk about in sermons. We are often more interested, better educated, and at times more articulate than other people. So what are we to do with all this? Are we not responsible for what we know? Do we not have a responsibility to share in the fullest ways possible the gift God has given to us? Do we not take the call of Romans 10:14-15 seriously and preach so that all might hear and believe?

To all of these questions I say yes. That's why we need to move beyond speaching. Progressional dialogue is a better way to share what we know with others. If Shelley truly wants to help the people she's talking to—and she does—then she has a responsibility to understand how they live, what their challenges are, and how they're affected by the knowledge she shares with them. Shelley's words will have a greater impact when she engages in the particularities of her listeners' lives than if she simply sets the agenda for what they talk about through one-way presentations.

For many of us our years of preparation are being underutilized in speaching; we know and believe more than can be shared in any speaching act. But we will flourish in settings where there is dialogue, where we become part of the learning and growing process of our congregations—not just as leaders, but as people who are also learning and growing—in ways we never imagined possible.

CHAPTER 5

HOW I BECAME A SPEACHER

While, when viewed in the broader scope of things, preaching has only recently turned into speaching, I find that congregations have quickly become socialized to accept speaching as the norm. In fact, the oddity of speaching and its effect on those listening was one of the first things I noticed about church life when I became a Christian.

My introduction into Christianity at age 16 came not through a sermon but by watching a passion play at a friend's church. Knowing nothing of Christianity, I felt as if the story told in this play seemed to creep inside every facet of my life almost instantly. The story simultaneously filled and consumed me. It was as if there was some calling on my life, some reorienting force, some—as I now call it—new implication for my life.

Within days of being "rearranged" I bought a Bible and started my way through it. I met with the adult leaders of a wonderful Christian youth organization who cared for and loved me. I began telling my story to my friends, most of whom were also unfamiliar with Christianity, and we began attending a small, conservative (not that I knew that at the time) church near my home. For an entire summer we attended the Sunday evening service; the Sunday morning service seemed to be at such an odd time that we never even thought of going then.

The pastor of this church would deliver in-depth speaches each Sunday night. Not knowing any better, I viewed this more as a conversation than a speach, and it showed. My friends and I would sit in the front row because we thought we should be close to the person with whom we were in conversation. We put our feet on the railing and listened, whispered to each other, wrote notes in our Bibles (which some of the folks of that church later told us was not a very good idea), and sometimes talked out loud about what was being said. At the end of the service we'd talk to Pastor Tucker about what he'd said and incorporate it all into our thinking.

But I also began to notice that almost none of the other people in the church—the regulars—seemed as interested in what the pastor was saying. Or if they were interested, they didn't seem to listen with the same attitude. We were listening as though this were a dialogue; they were listening as though it were a public address. They seemed content to just sit there and take it. We were in the front row feeling like we were integrated participants, as though Pastor Tucker were talking directly to us. We felt as if his words had great implication in our lives; the others seemed to view them as little more than thoughtful suggestions. To use the language of this book—it was preaching to us and speaching to them.

As it turned out, my impression may have been right. Pastor Tucker left the church shortly after we started attending. The rumor was that he was too lenient with us "outsiders" and didn't intervene in appropriate ways. Did I mention that on some Sundays we'd spend the afternoon swimming and then come to church in tank tops and swimsuits?

I don't say this in a judgmental way. It's my impression that most of that church would agree wholeheartedly with my assessment. In fact, it was that very thing that bothered them. They had the habitual responses to speaching and believed them to be the only acceptable responses. They wanted us to be better church people, ones who knew how to sit and listen to a sermon. Pastor Tucker would regularly comment to me how glad he was that we were at the church and that we shouldn't worry about what the other people were saying. Worry? I didn't even understand what they were saying. It was only after Pastor Tucker resigned and we were asked to leave the church (kicked out of my first church at age 17!) that I became aware that so many parishioners were uneasy with our unorthodox, "irreverent" listening practices.

Not long after that the leaders of the youth organization I was involved in starting putting me into situations where I talked in front of the group. I assumed most people would listen the way my friends and I did at our first church—the way I interacted with people all the time. We so infrequently interact with people in speech-giving settings that I assumed one should preach in the same way one talked. People began to tell me that my preaching "style" was conversational. I remember thinking, *Style? This is not a style. I thought we were having a conversation!*

Keep in mind that there was no actual conversation happening in either of these settings. It's not as though Pastor Tucker would say something and one of us would interject our response from the front pew. And in the youth organization there was still a designated time when I was the only one speaking. But even at that early age I knew a conversation didn't need to involve instant feedback to be interactive. I understood that simply having a posture of respect for the ideas and experiences of others and an attitude that said I expected feedback created—for me at least—an atmosphere of conversation.

Having a gift for evangelism and public speaking led me into leadership and speaking roles. I began speaking at churches, camps, weeknight meetings, Gospel Mission centers, and prisons. It was quite a shock to find that many of these groups had little interest in understanding the sermon as part of a larger communal conversation.

At first I thought the issue was that I was, for the most part, speaking to strangers. I wondered why these people would listen to a stranger on such important issues of faith. I assumed that their seeming lack of interest in offering feedback or engaging with what I was saying was due to the fact that we didn't have an established relationship. But I was soon told that it was not the person speaking but the act and the content that mattered to many of these people.

They had learned to dehumanize the speaker and focus on the words.

I'm not suggesting that the person should become more important than the message (that's how cults get started). But it seems to me we need to recognize and value the person and the relationship if the message is going to have any meaning in our lives.

Within three years of being introduced to Christianity I became an intern at a wonderful church with a tremendously gifted pastor who created a preaching environment that approached the feel of conversation. Because I felt like such a part of that community, the sermons seemed to come from someone I knew and respected, rather than being those removed, generic speeches created in private and delivered to the masses.

But that was not the case for most people. For many in the congregation this was a one-way interaction with a stranger. There were people in our church—regular attendees, mind you—who wouldn't refer to the pastor by his first name. They would gladly and regularly listen to him speach each week, but they never considered him a friend or peer; he was the pastor. No one was complaining about this arrangement; they didn't see anything wrong with it. In fact, they came by the thousands.

During this time I began to wonder if the kind of communities we create dictate the way we listen and if the way we listen dictates the kind of communities we become.

At this point I also noticed the amount of support that was given to make the stranger-preacher powerful. The platform, the microphone, the pulpit, the lights, the direction of the seating—all of it allowed the stranger to speak from a place of power. Interestingly, many churches have shifted their collective worship settings from dedicated buildings to homes in an effort to compensate for this seeming imbalance in power. (I am hesitant to call them "house churches" because I know true house churches are more than churches meeting in houses.) But often, because they haven't changed the intended outcome of the sermon, they also haven't changed the practices. So they still use the support systems of the dedicated building setting even after they move to the house; all the furniture is rearranged to face a small lectern or music stand at one end of the room, and there might even be a portable sound system to make sure the person speaching can be heard. Frankly, speaching makes these systems necessary. Street corner evangelists are a sad example of trying to do speaching without all the support. It rarely works.

There has only been a brief period in my adult life when I was not a pastor. During those two years I was engaged in ministry but went to church like a regular person. I cannot begin to describe how much this affected my thinking on preaching. Being on the other side can do that to a person.

For the first time I felt like an outsider, and I hated it. It was nothing the church did wrong that led to these feelings; it was all the things they did right. It was a wonderful church, and I really liked the pastor—as a preacher and as a person. The sermons were thoughtful and well put together. The pastor didn't talk down to us or come across as judgmental. But it still felt weird to me. But once again it didn't seem like anyone else minded. Since I liked the pastor, I tried to just sit there and keep my comments to Shelley to a minimum. I always brought my Bible so I could dig around for other things while the sermon was going on. I found my mind wanted to move faster and to more things than the sermon allowed. But mostly, I hated feeling like I was on the outside and the sermon was put together with a wide audience in mind. I understood the reasons for this; I had put sermons together for strangers, too. But being on the other side—being the nameless, faceless congregant—I felt like a victim of a random drive-by sermon. It wasn't intended for me; it wasn't created with me in mind. I just happened to be there that morning.

The cumulative effect of this kind of alienation, this sense of being perpetually on the outside, was hard for me to take. How much more alienating is our speaching to those who find it difficult to stay invested in a church in the face of these feelings, to those who are aching for connections and community?

CHAPTER 6

MY WAKE-UP CALL

Part of my issue with speaching is that I have come to see it as a subtle form of manipulation. Much of my training showed me how important it is for the speaching act to touch the emotions of the congregation. This was as essential to an effective sermon as sound exegesis. And I became adept at both.

I began to recognize the underside of all this in the mid-'90s. I'd been the senior high pastor at a suburban megachurch for several years, and I often spoke at camps. I'd created a regular repertoire of camp talks, knowing the point of a camp talk is to help center the campers' thinking on issues of God, at least during the chapel sessions. I also understood that this is incredibly difficult in a place where there are 300 to 500 hormone-ridden teenagers who are very much focused on other things. On top of that, teenagers have extraordinary "cool sensors" and don't automatically care what the camp speaker has to say. Building trust and becoming accepted by hundreds of students during a 30-minute chapel talk is a special kind of challenge. So once I found a few combinations of stories and biblical ideas that worked, it was hard to let go of them. And I have to admit I was very good at this. People often come up to me now—nearly a decade since I left youth ministry—because they remember hearing me speak, and they can tell me exactly what I said and how it impacted them.

One summer I took Ryan, a student from our ministry, along with me to a weeklong camp. He was interested in ministry and knew how to run a soundboard. On our way to the camp Ryan asked what I was going to talk about. I told him that at the first session, when my credibility was on the line, I'd use my "relationships change things" story. This was a true story about our youth group's spring break trip to Florida. I'd share about hundreds of kids hanging out at the beach, parasailing and renting motorcycles, and finish this part with a great story about bungee jumping. Then I'd talk about a student who was on that trip and how, two days after we returned home, he went into his garage, turned on his RX7, closed the door, and killed himself.

I really did feel the story was appropriate, that it brought important issues to the surface and made the point that I understood the pressure students were under and just how desperate and depressed they could feel. It also paved the way for me to spend the rest of the week talking about how there has to be more to an experience like spring break or camp than fun and friendship—there has to be a relationship with God.

I told Ryan he'd almost be able to taste the energy in the room when I finished with the bungee jumping story and that every kid would be with me. I told him to pay attention to how they would feel like they'd been hit in the stomach when I finished with the story of the boy's suicide. "Watch," I told him.

The talk went just as I predicted. Just after telling the story, with the room in a collective gasp, I glanced over at Ryan with a knowing look. We agreed with our eyes that it worked. But I had this sickening feeling in my stomach, a feeling that haunts me to this day. As I stood there, I realized that just because I can use a speech with a powerful story to lead a group where I want them to go, that doesn't mean I should. Knowingly manipulating the emotions of my hearers to get them to come to a predetermined conclusion felt like the very thing a pastor shouldn't do. It felt like a violation of the human relationship.

But I was conflicted. This style of preaching seemed to work. The students listened to me and, I think, were helped by what they heard. Still, the more I spoke in these settings, the more uncomfortable I became. I didn't know these students, even though I acted and sounded like I knew exactly where they were coming from. I didn't know what was happening in their homes, their schools, or their hearts. But I could compare their lives to a sinking boat where the water was rising faster than they could empty it, describe the sensation they felt of silently going under, and they believed I was one of the few adults who "got" them.

The students believed me; they believed I understood them and cared for them. And to some extent this was true. I wanted to help them, and maybe in this limited setting I was doing so. But as I considered this practice as a regular part of my life at my church, my concern and apprehension grew.

CHAPTER 7

A LOW-GRADE FEVER

Throughout this book I will use strong language to talk about issues related to speaching. But it's important to keep in mind that I see the problem of speaching as more of a low-grade fever than a medical emergency. Still it seems clear that this is not a sustainable way for the church to minister to its people. I have come to believe there's a kind of dehumanizing effect when week after week competent people aren't allowed to share their ideas and understanding; when week after week one person is set apart from the rest as the only one who is allowed to speak about God; when week after week people willingly, or by some sort of social or spiritual pressure, just sit and take it; when week after week they're taught that the only way to be good learners is to be better listeners.

Even when pastors agree that there is a problem, even when they sense their preaching isn't working the way they'd like it to, many are hesitant to place the blame on the speaching act itself. Instead they buy into one of the four main reasons given by most preaching resources—and most preachers—to explain the diminished impact of preaching.

The problem is the people. This argument is based on the idea that when speaching doesn't change lives, it's because the hearers are more concerned with advancing their own agendas than with being in tune with God's agenda. This self-centeredness leads people to become closed off to the Word of God and to the ways in which we are calling them into a new life. We try to woo them back with admonitions to repent and humble themselves before God, but they remain hard-hearted and unwilling to change.

I find this an odd argument to make against people who willingly go to church every week. Truly disinterested, hard-hearted people just don't go to church. When people show up, we need to view that as a testimony to their willingness to try and their genuine desire to have their faith make a difference in their lives.

The problem is the method. This reason is actually a more gracious form of "the problem is the people" explanation, in that it doesn't directly blame the individual for the failure of speaching. Rather it places the blame on the ways in which people in general have changed. The argument is that we live in a fast-paced culture where people have been conditioned only to take in "sound bites." The solution is for people to move beyond this cultural construct so they can develop a richer faith.

This perspective is at the heart of all sorts of preaching resources designed to "help engage this generation in worship." There is a new surge of books on preaching to the postmodern generation in which the focus is on the ways postmodernity has changed not only the culture but also the people, leading them to demand, even require, information in new ways. These books suggest bringing more mystery into worship with lighting, ready-made dramas, or sermon illustrations prefabbed into snappy PowerPoint®-like presentations. At a recent pastors' event I received a CD of preaching tips. One of the bonus tracks was entitled "Keeping Funeral Sermons Fresh." I understand there are many pastors who need to perform multiple funerals each month for their aging congregations, but it struck me as sad that our desire for the "right" material presented in the "right" way has extended to funerals.

The problem with this reasoning is that, for the most part, people—postmodern or otherwise—are able to take in much more information than any generation in history. It's simply untrue that people need their information in small, bite-sized or even "prechewed" pieces. The issue may not be that we have too much information or that we aren't presenting it in compelling ways, but perhaps the information we've chosen is not all that interesting. New methods and exciting delivery will do little to solve that problem. A better or more techno-savvy speech is still a speech.

The problem is the preacher. In talking with some pastors about the ineffectiveness of preaching, the conversation often comes around to the preacher's heart. If the preacher isn't passionately engaged with the Lord, then the preaching will be flat. Since this view tells us we can't take people any further than we ourselves have gone, then the pastor must make sure she is continually growing in her faith to have a deep well from which to preach.

This argument is the heart of a book called *Sermon Maker: Tales of a Transformed Preacher* by Calvin Miller, whom I deeply respect. While I so appreciate the author, I find this reasoning to be wanting; it simply doesn't match reality. There are too many stories of preachers who felt they had no "deep well" from which to give, and yet their sermons were incredibly powerful. There are also too many stories of preachers who were so in the groove with God that God's desires and theirs seemed indistinguishable, and yet their sermons fell on deaf ears.

This reasoning rubs me wrong on a personal level as well, for I find myself needing to be transformed by the people I am preaching to. I would much rather walk with them than act as their pace car. If the role of the preacher is to be the one who has arrived so he can give hope to those who are lagging behind, then we are in serious trouble. There is no amount of personal passion or holiness that can undo the effects of speaching.

The problem is the content. This view has increased in popularity in recent years, especially in "emergent-esque" communities. It argues that speaching falls short because we're saying the wrong things. There are variations on these wrong messages. For some it's too much "personal gospel"; for others it's a message lacking in care for the poor. And still others believe it's selling the story short, selling out, or just plain selling.

In other circles the problem is seen not as the content failing to include all that it should, but that the content has grown to include too much. In his book *Post-Rapture Radio: Lost Writings from the Failed Revolution at the End of the Last Century,* my friend Russell Rathbun brilliantly argues this point, saying we've missed the subversive nature of the story of Jesus. If we would return to that message and get away from the consumerist Americana story, we would once again know speaching in all its glory.

While I agree that we need to make these adjustments and that our message must become the subversive, prophetic story of the kingdom, this still doesn't solve the problem of speaching. We must pursue new practices as well as new messages; the two are inseparable. It won't suffice to put new ideas in the trappings of old practices. When we offer a new message through a practice designed to propagate a different message, we may well lose both.

This is not to say there is never a time for speaching, but I believe that for churches to maintain spiritual health, it should be a small part of the preaching repertoire, not the mainstay. Let me give you an example of what I mean. Over the last 10 years my family has shifted to an organic, natural diet. We eat meat, but usually as a side dish and not the main course. We believe a healthy diet is centered on fruits, vegetables, and whole grains, with meat included in smaller portions. Still we recognize there is a place for meat in our diet, especially living in Minnesota where the weather is often cold and the protein in meat is quite beneficial. There may be times when we need to go on a high-protein diet that will have certain short-term benefits, but it's not a healthy, lifelong practice.

There may be benefits to speaching as an occasional act, too. It can certainly serve as a way to get a conversation started. At Solomon's Porch we recently spent some time working through issues relating to financial giving to our community. We began the process with a meeting where people could say their pieces about tithing, finances, and so on. Then we decided to spend a month or so considering our own lives on this issue before coming back together to continue the dialogue.

I once worked at a church where we had a tradition of meeting for a Maundy Thursday service each Easter season. The service had a serious, contemplative tone to it. Presentations were made, music was sung, and we were dismissed in silence. Watching a few thousand people walk out of the building in near silence was an extremely powerful experience. In this setting the best way for us to respond was to remain in the quietness.

Interestingly, both of these examples of appropriate speaching still include some form of response from the hearers. While in one case it's several weeks of discernment and in the other it's silence, there is still a sense in which the agenda is handed over to the people of the congregation, and they're allowed to add or take from it what they will.

CHAPTER 8

GENERIC MESSAGES

Speaching is a violation of what we know about building relationships. Speaching isn't the normal way to talk or listen, and it isn't the normal way to build trust or community. It is, in fact, best suited for promoting a generic message for a generic audience.

I was recently driving behind a car with a bumper sticker that read, "Hang up and drive." It struck me that far more people who aren't using their cell phones while driving will see that sticker each day than those who are on phones. So the person in this car is telling people they should stop doing something they probably aren't even doing. She took her desire for people not to use their cell phones while driving and turned it into a statement made to everyone driving behind her.

I thought about how strange it is to tell people things based on your desires about the way you want the world to be, rather than finding out more about what's important in the lives of other people. I found myself saying, "I'm not even on the phone. Why are you giving me instructions that have nothing to do with my situation?" I concluded that the bumper sticker is really her chance to get something off her chest, not a message to any person's specific situation. She probably felt better because she was able to share her opinion about people using cell phones while they drive. Whether or not it had anything to do with the life of the person right behind her wasn't the point.

When the content of the sermon is created in the isolated setting of the pastor's mind and study and is delivered to whomever happens to be at church that Sunday, it has all the impact of that bumper sticker. The speacker may feel he's said his piece and mistake that for having preached the gospel. But the gospel isn't generic good news; it's particular good news. It's good news in the life of the people who hear it and seek to live it out as a community of faith.

Jenell is a woman in our church who suffered a devastating loss when her triplet sons were born very prematurely, unable to survive. The death of her children has reshaped her life in ways no one can fathom. For someone like Jenell, progressional dialogue is a way for her to continue processing what's happened in her life within the context of a community she loves and trusts. Not long ago she blogged about her impressions of a Sunday night sermon. While she did not make this blog post with this book in mind, she did give me permission to share it here.

> Last night's sermon was about Jesus in Mark—feeding the 4,000, feeding the 5,000, spitting twice in the blind man's eyes, and then Peter misunderstanding Jesus—"get behind me, Satan." The sermon and subsequent discussion seemed to focus on how both the Pharisees and disciples misunderstood Jesus'

message, expecting a messianic earthly kingdom instead of a Messiah who would die in order to bring them some other kind of kingdom. Several people said the application to them was that they need to set aside their agenda and their sense of how God works and let God be God.

I reacted to this sermon first by nearly falling asleep—I dozed off a few times, but I think I caught most of what was going on. I dress too warmly for our warm church and then get tired. More to the point of this blog, however, I felt both angry and safe. Many Christians interpret these passages to mean that the Jews were selfish idiots who just wanted power, but we Christians understand the message perfectly. At the Porch, of course, we are more likely to question the ways in which we still misunderstand the message. Either way I don't like it. The Jews were an oppressed minority in an empire, and they had experienced God's earthly salvation from slavery in the past. They weren't being selfish idiots to expect it again. They knew by heart God's actions in the past, and they were being faithful as best they knew how. And what use is an eternal kingdom to people who are suffering in the present? It is, of course, of ultimate value to those who have eyes to perceive and ears to hear, but it's an incredibly difficult saying.

And if we today still don't get the message, then what is God doing? If the message is so important, why doesn't he communicate it in a way that is more understandable? And if he cares so much for his creation, why doesn't he save them from slavery and oppression? The kingdom message is foolish in both of these ways—it does not address "felt needs," and it is not as clear as you'd think something so important would be. It's an offense.

I know I'm a fool for being offended by the gospel, but it makes me angry. Like the Jews, I have some pretty desperate wants in this life, and it's hard to let them go and receive instead what God is really offering. I can see why people in stories sell their souls to the devil. They're willing to barter the future to alleviate the unbearable reality of the present. There have been days when I'd do it if I could.

It's hard to understand Jesus' power when he doesn't use it to solve very obvious, immediate, and pressing problems. What good is a Messiah who will die when the Jews needed freedom in the moment? What good is eternal life for me when I just want my family intact in this life? I have a list of demands, and many days eternal life, peace, rest, and clear spiritual perspective are way down the list. Raise my dead for me, and then I'll listen to your other yammerings, Jesus.

When people at church talked about setting aside their agendas for God's, I was alarmed. Do we know what we're saying? For me the challenge is to hold my loved ones while I have them and let them go when they go. Release my children to God, knowing I never get to hold them or love them again in this life. Trust that I ought to choose to stay alive because God will still fill my life with goodness, peace, and love. Live today in peace and joy, even though I know full well how bad things have been and how bad they may be again. Die to self? I would rather have really died last year than to, these days, wake up and work again to be grateful for the life I have instead of to be bitter over what I don't have. That, for me, is dying to self. It really feels like dying, except it happens every day instead of being a once-and-for-all physical death.

The reward, on my better days, is a life of inappropriate joy. A bereaved mother shouldn't be happy, but I am happy. I shouldn't enjoy earthly pleasures, but I do enjoy food, warmth, sleep, and cats. I see my life and the lives of my sons for what they are. Life is extremely valuable but transient. It is worth everything today, but it may be gone tomorrow. All I can do is love and live in the present, without worry for the future. Live without being hounded by the bad past or terrified by the potentially bad future. Live like the birds of the air or the lilies of the field.

Jesus spit once in the blind man's eyes, and he saw people walking around who looked like trees. He spit a second time, and the man both saw stuff and correctly perceived what it was. God, spit in my eyes twice today and every day so I can see *and* perceive, hear *and* understand.

—Excerpted with permission from *jenellparis. blogspot.com*

I can't imagine Jenell, or anyone else, having to sit through a generic sermon on God's faithfulness offered by someone more concerned about the church agenda than the real experience of the people listening. I can't imagine any preacher arrogant enough to presume to know how Jenell and her husband should live in light of their grief and pain.

CHAPTER 9

PREACHING FROM A STRANGER

I recently met a man at an art show. While we were talking, the topic of what we each did for a living came up. When I told him I was a pastor, he said, "Really? Wow, I don't get to talk to many pastors." I assumed he meant he didn't go to church very often. So when he said, "I've been a member of a large local Baptist church for 11 years," I was surprised. Somewhat confused, I asked, "You've been part of the church for 11 years and don't talk to your pastor?" He replied, "Well, I hear what my pastor says, but I don't ever talk to him like this. He's really important and works hard to create the material for his sermons on Sundays, and I wouldn't want to bother him or take up his time."

I wish his was a unique experience, but it's not. No matter the size of the church, speaching often creates an environment in which the pastor remains a removed stranger who gives speeches about God.

There are some situations when it's preferable to be involved with a stranger. And by "stranger" I mean someone I know but who is not a regular part of my life and with whom my contact is almost exclusively centered on a specific task. I have friends who are really great massage therapists, but I still prefer to get a massage from a stranger. The same is true for the people who cut my hair. But this is not the case for playing golf, going to movies, or riding on public transportation—those are things I prefer to do with my friends.

It seems to me that faith formation is one of those things that ought to happen in the company of friends. If someone is going to speak into the most essential and intimate parts of my life, it seems that person ought to know who I am and vice versa. But here again we have socialized our congregations to expect far less than what is possible.

I was once a guest speaker at a youth ministry event for a large church. Before my time to speak I sat down among the thousand or so students. I asked a girl I didn't know, and who didn't know I was the speaker, if I could sit next to her. She gave me that typical 16-year-old response of, "Yeah, sure, I guess." I tried to make small talk by introducing myself, but she wasn't at all interested, so the small talk came to an end. After a few minutes of music and announcements I was introduced and went to the stage to give my talk. (Interestingly, in youth ministry the sermon is often referred to as a "talk," for a sermon isn't what most youth ministries are getting at. The use of the word *talk* exemplifies the desire for this to be something more than a speech, even though rarely it is.) Afterward that girl came up to me and said, "I can't believe you were sitting right next to me. I've never met one of the speakers here. I know my team leader, but I've only been around for two years and haven't met any of the main stage people before, and there you were sitting right next to me." Here she was, just 16 and already expected to have little to no relationship with the people entrusted with her spiritual formation.

This is not only the case in large groups. About the same time we were starting Solomon's Porch, I was an interim pastor for a church of about 150 people. I preached there in the morning and at Solomon's Porch in the evening. Perhaps it was because I was just the fill-in guy for nine months, or maybe I wasn't perceived as all that approachable, but in those nine months only a handful of people ever engaged me in meaningful conversation despite my efforts to get to know them. They didn't seem to see anything abnormal about having a stranger join them on Sunday and give speeches about God. They were oddly satisfied with me—a total stranger—stepping into the pulpit each week. They seemed to feel about me the way I feel about my massage therapist: You can help me, even touch me, but that's the extent of this relationship. I can't imagine this is how we want our congregations to feel about us, but this is precisely the relationship created by speaching.

When I preach at other churches, I often compare the experience to a blind date. I tell them how odd I find this practice. I tell them I recognize that for the next chunk of time we are going to do something together as strangers that is normally done within a relationship, that the way this is supposed to work is that I would know them and they would know me. I explain that normally you go on dates with people you know and trust and feel safe with, but for this date we'll fake it and act like we know one another. We'll do things that make it seem like we have a relationship, fully recognizing that we don't. And I tell them that I'm the worst kind of date: I'll do all the talking. But the good news is, I probably won't call them for a second date, so if they can tough it out for a bit, they'll never have to see me again.

The reason I use this analogy is not only to break the ice or to only bring into the open the oddity of listening to strangers for our spiritual guidance. The real reason is to plant a prophetic seed, a reminder that settling for this kind of preaching is not our only option.

CHAPTER 10

PREACHING TO STRANGERS

Because most of the other churches where I speak are set up around the speaching model, I find I need to keep those skills intact. But it's a hard transition from what I am growing used to at my church, for I find myself being transformed by the practice of progressional dialogue as much as anyone else in our community. In fact, the greatest transformation from progressional preaching may happen in the preacher.

When I was a youth pastor and new to the whole preaching experience, I was given several wonderful opportunities to preach during the main services. It was an honor and also served to stretch and shape me. On a fairly regular basis I preached at the service during the infamous week between Christmas and New Year's Day, also known as "the wasteland." It's the Sunday that just can't compete with Christmas on one side and New Year's on the other. Christmas steals all the religious thunder, and New Year's Day gets dibs on the "it's time to make big life changes" sermon.

But the greatest struggle with "wasteland Sunday" is that you don't know who'll be at church. It all depends on where Christmas fell during the week—people might still be out of town. Even if they're around, they may have had their fill of church in the last month, and Wasteland Sunday is the perfect time to take a little break. If they show up, they may come with extended family in tow, meaning you're part of the vacation package and you'd better deliver.

I was always grateful for the chance to preach, but Wasteland Sunday makes tough work for the novice. I remember a number of Saturday nights and Sunday mornings spent wondering if what I had put together would have any connection to the people who would show up for church that day. It was the epitome of the stranger speaching to the stranger. At youth events I knew the hearers at least shared a common age range so I could speak to their "youthfulness" and feel like I was connecting. At an outreach event I could speak to the lostness of people. But Wasteland Sunday was an odd mix of people, some who wanted to be there and some who did not.

This was readily apparent from my place on the platform. As was the custom at this church the preacher came out and sat on the platform when the service began. So there I was sitting alone and staring at the faces of the people. It was during this time that I would see it dawn on people that the regular pastor wasn't there and they were going to hear from a fill-in. Some would smile at me and sort of say "Hi." Others would smile and sort of say, "Sorry they make you sit up there like a disciplined school child." But others would nearly sprain their necks while quickly looking to their bulletins and hoping their fears would not be confirmed in print—that on this Sunday they wouldn't have to hear from the fill-in.

The pressure to deliver a good message was intense. It was hard to come up with material to connect with this broad collection of people. But the speaching must go on. I knew it and they knew it. Fortunately, this church had very gracious people, so we always managed to get through these Sundays with no harm done. But it was during these experiences that I started to wonder about the legitimacy of what we all considered "normal." I wondered about the benefit to the people and the effect on me.

CHAPTER 11

IMPLICATION VS. APPLICATION

I am by no means suggesting our sermons are meaning-less. As I said early in this book, I believe preaching to be a biblical part of the life of the church. In fact, it is precisely because sermons *do* have meaning that we need to reconsider the ways in which we create and use them in the context of our communities.

The sermon is often thought of as the "practical" part of church. It's the point where we as pastors are asked to take the sometimes-difficult-to-understand Bible and bring it to life for our congregations. Every pastor I know truly wants those hearing the sermon to get something from it, to somehow take it home and be affected by it. We want our sermons to live on in the lives of our people, to know they are being changed week by week. It is my contention that speaching prevents this from happening, primarily because speaching is centered on application, *not implication*.

The idea that sermons should serve as lessons for applying God's truth to our lives is a hard one to overcome. Even people who've taken part in our progressional preach-ing still ask me about the "take-away" of the sermon. They want a point or two they can cling to as they leave our space and head out into the world. After one Sunday gathering I received this e-mail from a man who is very open to what we're doing but who is still caught in the application model (even though you'll see he is perfectly capable of finding the implications on his own):

> This is Eric, the bald guy/goatee, who came with his beautiful brunette seriously dating girlfriend Beth for the first time yesterday. I have two questions. First, I really enjoyed your talk on Mark 8. Are you working your way through Mark right now at church? Or are you doing some other series?
>
> Second, both of us received great new insight from your message and I enjoyed listening to others' thoughts. However, I was disappointed you didn't wrap or sum up the comments of the congregation. Is there a reason you didn't? Is that your style or something you do on occasion?
>
> I really think it's awesome that you include discussion in the church service, but since you are the pastor and our shepherd in regards to Solomon's Porch (although we're all leaders and ministers in the larger scheme of things), I desire to hear you help us understand why there are different takes on the message or to connect them together in a way that we can have some take-home message. I understand that it is important as a church to expand our way of thinking and ways which we incorporate Scripture into our lives and the lives of others, but I also believe that whenever we open the Word, there is absolute

truth that stands out that we all need to grasp. I feel like yesterday the truth may have been the idea that we, as Christ's disciples, need to transform our lives by first ridding ourselves of all earthly preconceptions we have of Christ and Christianity (as Paul writes in Cor. 5, to get rid of our old "yeast") in order that we may follow and serve him in truth (or more clearly, as with the second healing of the blind man). I feel that I need to hear from my pastor, wherever I go, some suggestions of how to apply this in a real way to my life. Perhaps you did and I missed it, and I apologize if I did. Otherwise I felt like there was a vague take-home message. Thank you dearly for any response you can offer.

The practice of applying Scripture to our lives is not the established Christian tradition but rather the product of more recent ways of thinking about church. Our post-Enlightenment ways of thinking move us to want answers rather than more questions, to seek instant take-away rather than long processes, to seek out solutions rather than ponder the problem itself. We have, over the last century, become people who believe in answers and application. We have little patience for ambiguity or uncertainty. As a result the question of the church has increasingly become, "What does the Bible have to do with my life today?" This question has become so all-encompassing that the success of a church is often measured by the pastor's ability to answer that question.

The emphasis on application is also apparent in the Christian publishing industry, which has been thriving in recent years, primarily because of the increasing publication of "practical" Bible study materials meant to address specific life issues, daily devotionals and prayer journals with tidy prayers and fill-in-the-blanks learning tools, and even Bibles themselves created to be applicable to certain demographic groups. While these might be perfectly helpful to many people, it seems to me that if these products were truly creating the kind of life-altering spiritual formation we'd like them to create in the millions of people who purchase them, the church would be changing the world in a way no one could miss—not in the sense of swinging an election or having a voice in the public forum but in bringing about the kingdom of God, one in which God's peace and justice and compassion reign.

While it has become our default method of making Scripture practical, application is actually quite tricky. One must find ways to tell other people how this thing they didn't know about is really important to their lives, yet they needed an outsider to point it out to them. We have to tell them this with passion and gravity but at the same time avoid coming across as superior. Those of us who preach regularly know just how delicate we must be and many times fear we have either overstepped or understepped. We preachers rarely feel we get this just right, and I suspect our congregations feel much the same way. Even when pastors try to stand alongside their congregations in a place of application, they risk one of two messages: Either the pastor has already applied it, which heightens the judgmental feeling, or the pastor hasn't gotten there yet, which makes the listener wonder, "If she can't do it, what chance do I have?"

Preaching as progressional dialogue calls for a different reaction from those who hear a sermon. Where application asks, "Do you see what I see?" or, "Do you know what I know?" implication asks, "What do we do now?" Application has a sense of *me* to it; implication has a sense of *us*. Rather than going off to our separate cars where we may or may not discuss the sermon with our families, we are asked to talk about what we're hearing together. Rather than splitting into small groups of people who are usually very much like us, we are asked to consider the implications of God's Word for us as God's diverse people.

This difference is crucial to the ways in which we understand ourselves as God's people. Application allows us to remain disconnected, to think of our faith in individualistic terms. But nowhere in the Bible do we see faith as an individual endeavor. It is always a communal practice. Even the stories about people of faith—Moses, David, Job—are told from a communal perspective; the point is never what happens *to* them but what happens *because of* them. The sense of us that comes through implication opens our communities to the notion that we aren't simply people who gather once a week for a common experience, but we are part of something bigger than ourselves. Suddenly, we tap into the power of the community to be a source of formation, of life change. Implication takes down the walls that exist between the people in our communities and allows us to be vulnerable with one another as we share in the journey of faith. It moves us to connect with other people who have been down this road. Think about the ways in which the disciples responded whenever they listened to Jesus preach. They wondered what this call would mean for them. They talked to each other about what they'd heard. They asked Jesus questions about how his words were changing them. They were not asking questions of application, but of reorientation.

At the same time, implication causes people to take their own faith seriously. It's a much deeper question to ask how we fit into the story of God than to ask what we're supposed to do with the story. In truth, implication is the more instinctive response to a powerful story. This is the sense people have when they see a movie. Scary movies are scary because viewers tend to see themselves as part of the story or believe the story could become a part of their lives. There is an entire generation of moviegoers who cannot enter the shower without thinking about the shower scene from *Psycho*. Even children begin to develop coping mechanisms for scary movies, telling themselves or being told, "It's just a movie; it's not real."

I've been in so many conversations where someone, quite often me, makes a movie or television show reference to connect or explain a situation. This connection is implicatory. We sense that what happened there is what is also happening here. Preaching ought to build in us the ability to weave our lives with the multiple stories of our world. This is the idea behind the prophet Isaiah's words: "Do you not know? Have you not heard? The Lord is the everlasting God, the Creator of the ends of the earth. He will not grow tired or weary, and his understanding no one can fathom. He gives strength to the weary and increases the power of the weak" (Isaiah 40:28-29).

Many of us were taught that part of the purpose of the sermon is to make the Word of God accessible to people, to make it easier for them to understand and live into. Stop and think about that for a minute. Is that really what preaching is for? Is that how Jesus or Paul preached? Some would say Jesus used parables to make the gospel more accessible, but Jesus' hearers were often just as confused by the parables as they were by his other words. The purpose of preaching isn't to make the Word of God easy; it's to help people delve into faith more fully, more deeply.

Educational theory tells us people really only learn out of frustration—the frustration that they don't know but need to, the frustration that life isn't working but there could be a better way. Frustration is not a bad thing—it's a necessary thing. It's what pushes us on. In the story of Nathan and David (2 Samuel 12:1-13), Nathan tells David a story in order to confront David about his adulterous relationship with Bathsheba and the murder of her husband. Over the course of the story David's anger and frustration peak, leaving him in a place where he can finally see the true nature of his actions. Nathan's response of, "You are the man!" is classic implication. He doesn't tell David what to do but rather leaves David with little choice but to rearrange his life because of what he has heard.

Implication destabilizes. When a person is told she has cancer or she's won the lottery or her house burned down, she instantly recognizes she's in a new situation and a new story. While her initial reaction might be one of application (*What will I do now?*), she quickly moves into implication (*How will this change me and the life I live?*) Application is about how a piece of information fits into your life. Implication is not about fitting; it's about redefining. It's not value-added suggestion; it's a call to see the story and join in it.

The story of the transfiguration is an incredible one in so many ways, including how poorly the disciples who were present understood what was happening. After returning from the mountain, the disciples were becoming increasingly aware that Jesus was going to experience a prophet's end. They began to work on their succession plan, trying to figure out who among them was the greatest. A bit later James and John came right out and asked if they could be the next in command. (Mark 9) While their understanding was skewed, they knew that Jesus' story about what would happen to him involved them as well, and they were trying to figure out how to organize their lives in light of it.

The story of the Bible and the Christian faith doesn't lend itself well to the listen-and-apply model. In fact, this may well be the reason so many of the "hard to understand" sections of the Bible are often ignored in our churches. What do you say in an application-based speech after reading the story of Jephthah and his daughter in Judges 11? Perhaps there are broad, generic applications to be made, but it seems to me that Scripture is intended for more than that.

The good news is not informational. It's not a secret that only a few are meant to understand. It's a call to all—the educated and the simple, the informed and the out of touch. Certainly there are settings where a speech ought to precede application. The pharmacist should tell the patient the important information about the medicine, and the patient should listen carefully and follow the prescription. That's why it's called a prescription. But this is not the nature of the gospel. Instead we have an invitation into a way of life—a life we constantly realize is not ours alone. Ours is a story that is so all-consuming none of us can apply it and call our work done.

SECTION FOUR
WHY WE'RE RELUCTANT TO CHANGE

CHAPTER 12

HOLDING ON TO SPEACHING

I don't think we can change speaching without changing the assumptions that allowed for speaching in the first place. It wasn't by accident that the church ended up preaching through speech making. It was an intentional move by some, and others picked it up out of obligation or lack of an alternative. It's a practice with a significant background. The call to re-imagine preaching is also a call to re-imagine the assumptions that led us here.

The professionalization of ministry. The pastorate has changed dramatically over the centuries. Once primarily thought of as a calling, it's now often seen as a career. This professionalization of the pastorate has had an interesting impact on both pastors and parishioners. When some people first hear the idea of the community teaching one another, they will often ask the pastor, "Then what do we pay you for?" I know this statement is made because it's been made to me. At Solomon's Porch we've worked hard to create a culture where the leading of one another is not only the norm but also the expectation. Even so there are times when people say things that remind me of how entrenched we are in idea that the pastor is the professional in the things of faith.

In our church we use a Bible discussion group to help form the sermon. Most Sunday nights we make an announcement inviting people to join us on the upcoming Tuesday. One night Dustin, the announcement guy, was trying to keep things interesting, so he said something like, "Come on Tuesday and hear the sermon a few days early." For some reason I felt it would be good to remind people that the discussion group is a place to participate in the creation of the sermon, not hear me practice it and offer feedback. So I interrupted Dustin with a slight clarification. Then Dustin, who has one of the fastest minds I've ever known, said, "So on Tuesday come and help Doug do his job and then on Wednesday come to my work and help me do mine." The room exploded with laughter and applause. People got it. They know we're working to renegotiate the role—not only of the pastor, but of the community as well.

I've talked to medical doctors who are bothered by the amount of healthcare information that's available on the Internet. One doctor said, "I have a more difficult time doing my job when people come to me with a self-diagnosis and treatment plan already in mind. I'm the professional. They simply cannot learn what I know just because they look on the Internet." This frustration, while real to doctors, leaves them in the minority. People make better patients and healthier people when they're more involved in understanding their health. The medical profession must train doctors to know how to interact with the changing patient of the information age. Web portals like WebMD.com are here to stay, and people will continue to seek a more active role in their healthcare.

There are far too many pastors who take this same perspective—feeling threatened by the idea that regular people might have something to contribute to the spiritual formation of the community. But it's a *good* thing when people want to be more engaged in their spiritual lives. Look—churches will always need pastors, just as patients will always need doctors. Thus it's logical to expect that as the medical profession needs to adjust its expectations of its patients, the pastoral profession should also be willing to rethink the role of the parishioner in the life of the church.

Lack of options. I've talked with numerous pastors about preaching beyond speaching. While many of them are intrigued by the idea of trying something else, most stick with speaching because they can't come up with any other viable options.

Not long ago I gave a presentation to the students and faculty at the seminary from which I graduated—a scary endeavor, I can assure you. We talked about progressional preaching as an alternative to speaching. One of the attendees said, "This progressional preaching sounds really exciting, and I can see how it works with a few hundred people, but wouldn't there be chaos if you tried this with thousands?"

My first thought was, "Probably. So maybe we should reconsider the structures that put thousands of people in one room at the same time." But I didn't say that. Instead I went to my second thought, "Sure, it might create chaos, but is that really any worse than having thousands of people sitting there disconnected and uninvolved?" My third thought was perhaps more helpful. I told him we live in a time of the greatest human innovation ever. There are people living on a space station; others are manipulating the human genome. There are people creating whole new materials at the atomic level though nanotechnology. And there's evidence of human innovation at work in the church world as well. We've figured out how to move thousands of people into our church buildings for hour-long worship gatherings and then get them out in time to clear the parking lot before the next group of thousands arrives. We've developed sophisticated youth and adult ministries, and on our church staffs we have more people with advanced education degrees than ever before. We can certainly figure out workable ways to move preaching beyond speech making.

Speakers are rewarded. We live in a culture where people are respected and socially rewarded for being able to give a speech and even more so for giving a good speech. This is no less true in the church where the most well-known pastors are those who are great speakers, while those who excel at pastoral counseling or church administration rarely get their pictures on magazine covers.

The Internet is ripe with help for those who want to be better speech makers. Here is the text from one Web site (*www.amazingmethods.com/speech*):

Dear Friend:

I was a nobody. The girl I secretly admired

would not even glance at me. Others often made me the butt of jokes until one night at a party...

"Speech! Speech!" they again shouted, urging me to speak and hoping they would put me to shame, because they felt sure I'd rather jump from the rooftop of the building than deliver a speech!

I could hear the giggles and the whisper...then the silence.

But when I began speaking, I could see the whites of their eyes slowly widen.

From my first word I seized their attention. I made them laugh. I made them cry. I held them spellbound till my last word.

At the end of my speech there was thunderous applause, a standing ovation.

My great moment had come! Everyone flocked to me, even my boss. And the girl I secretly admired shook my hand, and I wished it were eternity!

They all asked me, "How did you learn to speak so well?"

They couldn't believe me when I said, "I learned everything I knew about public speaking while driving through traffic jams!" Before I explain—

LET ME ASK YOU A QUESTION:

Do you sometimes wish you could speak better and more effectively? Truly—

The person who speaks well commands attention, respect, love, and admiration WHEREVER HE GOES.

When he speaks, everybody listens. He can make you laugh. He can make you cry. He can inspire you to action. He has the power to move an audience of one or a thousand at will!

You've seen men like him. Wherever he goes, he commands attention and respect. When he talks, no one ignores him. He can hold you spellbound by the power of his words alone.

And he almost always gets what he wants: a high-paying job, a raise, a promotion, an election, higher grades, public support, and the respect and admiration of people he loves.

Honestly, do you sometimes wish you could speak like him? YOU CAN BE LIKE HIM!

I wonder if the social kudos given to those who are comfortable with public speaking is part of what keeps speaching an honored tradition in the church. Consider that when churches are interviewing potential pastors, the candidate is asked to preach a sample sermon. Not only does this communicate that the ability to deliver a strong speach is a requirement of the job, but it's also often the only part of the search process in which the broader church community takes part. Thus the congregation knows little about a new pastor apart from his strengths as a speacher. Unfortunately, we place such a high value on the ability to give a speech that this is often enough. The candidate who knocks us out with a great sermon is the one we want because he is the one who can transcend the fears of ordinary people and do something otherworldly.

No call to re-imagine it. The speaching view of preaching has so infiltrated the church that it is rarely questioned. But we are called to be people of re-creation, people who are constantly seeking to live in God's creative Spirit. The notion that speaching can and should be up for reform need not be seen as a threat or even as a course correction. Rather reformation ought to be part of our Christian character. Our churches should never be places where the practices of faith are allowed to become stagnant and predictable in the name of stability. The call to reimagine applies not only to the speaching act, but also to the way we serve communion, the way we pray, the way we are seated, the way we teach our children. Every part of our life as a community can and should be open to the fresh ideas of the always-active Spirit of God.

CHAPTER 13

THOSE FOR WHOM THIS CONVERSATION WILL SEEM UNNECESSARY

I was recently in a conversation with a good friend and pastor of an emergent-esque community. He strongly disagreed with my contention that speaching doesn't work. I suggested to him that those who lived during periods of time or in places where speaching was not the normative means of preaching (basically all people before the 1700s and those living in nonindustrialized settings in our day) were not adversely affected by the lack of speaches. He countered by saying, "That is just not true. The people before the Reformation were not well-taught, and that's why the church degraded to such an extent that the Reformation was necessary." His argument was that strong teaching done through speaching is still needed to keep the church from once again falling into a state that requires deep reformation.

For him speaching is not a problem for the church; it's the solution. While he agrees that speaching needs some repairs, he believes those fixes involve pastors learning to deliver speaches with greater connectedness, relevancy, and honesty. The idea that speaching itself might be worth rethinking is not one he considers.

He isn't the only one for whom this conversation will seem ill-conceived. There are those who are so wedded to preaching that they can hardly differentiate the function of the church from the practices of the church. There are really good, intelligent people who hold a view on the function of preaching in the church that is very different from mine. But I'm not trying to convince people that speaching is a failure as much as I'm trying to provide a new way of thinking for those who've already concluded such but don't have the words to go with their intuition.

In his 1972 book *Preaching & Preachers*, the master orator Dr. D. Martyn Lloyd-Jones makes a strong case for the primacy of speaching in the function of the church. Dr. Lloyd-Jones, who was by nearly all accounts brilliant, preached at Westminster Chapel from 1938 to 1968, and in the minds of many, he represents the finest in reformed preaching.

For Lloyd-Jones preaching as speaching is a sign of effective leadership. He contends that ineffective preaching is the result of preachers losing a necessary confidence in truth and unwittingly setting aside the crucial role of leading, one that is best accomplished by master orators. He says this:

> As preaching has waned, there has been an increase in the formal element in the service. They have argued that the people should have a greater part in the service, and so they have introduced "responsive reading" and more and more music and singing and chanting...It has been illuminating to observe

these things; as preaching has declined, these other things have been emphasized; and it has all been done quite deliberately. It is a part of this reaction against preaching; and people have felt that it is more dignified to pay this greater attention to ceremony, and form, and ritual. Still worse has been the increase in the element of entertainment in public worship—the use of films and the introduction of more and more singing; the reading of the Word and prayer shortened drastically, but more and more time given to singing...

This is a part of this whole depreciation of the message. Then on top of this, there is the giving of testimonies. It has been interesting to observe that as preaching as such has been on the decline, preachers have more and more used people to give their testimonies...This is deemed to be of much greater value than the preaching and the exposition of the Gospel. Have you noticed that I have put all this under the term *entertainment*? That is where I believe it truly belongs. But this is what the church has been turning to as she has turned her back upon preaching....

I am not attempting to deal with all the aspects of a minister's work but with preaching because I believe that this comes first and is most important. Visiting, or any other activity, can never compensate for a lack of preaching. Indeed I suggest that visiting will not have much meaning unless the preaching has been what it should be and has prepared the way.

But now, turning from what has happened in that way amongst those who still believe in the church, let us look at those who are more or less suggesting that the church herself may be the hindrance and that we have got to abandon the church if we really are to propagate the gospel. I am thinking here of those who say that we must, in a sense, make a clean break with all this tradition which we have inherited, and that if we really want to make people Christians, the way to do so is to mix with them, to live amongst them, to share our lives with them, to show the love of God to them by just bearing one another's burdens and being one of them.

I have heard this put in this way even by preachers.

So, they argue, if you really want to influence people in the Christian direction, you must not only *talk* politics and deal with social conditions in *speech* [italics mine], you must take an active part in them...A very well-known preacher in Britain actually put it like this some 10 years ago. He said that the idea of sending our foreign missionaries to North Africa...and training them to preach to these people was quite ridiculous, and it was time we stopped it. He suggested that instead we should send Christian people out to those places, and they should take on ordinary jobs, mix among the people, and more especially, enter into their political and social affairs. If you did that as Christians, he said, then there would be some hope perhaps that the grandchildren of this present generation might become Christian. But that was the way, you see, to do it. Not preaching, not the old method, but getting among the people, showing an interest, showing your sympathy, being one of them, sitting down among them, and discussing their affairs and problems.

Well now the great question is—what is our answer to all this? I am going to suggest, and this will be the burden of what I hope to say, that all this at best is secondary, very often not even secondary, often not worthy of a place at all, but at best secondary, and that the primary task of the church and of the Christian minister is the preaching of the Word of God.

—*Preaching & Preachers* (pp. 16-18, 185)

I won't take the time to refute the thoughts presented by Dr. Lloyd-Jones other than to say that his view of preaching, while well-articulated, bears little resemblance to mine and to further suggest that those who are convinced of his position are not likely to find value in my ideas about preaching. If one were convinced of his perspective, one might be better served by drawing from the vast resources devoted to refining the role of Reformed preaching than spending time in this book. (This might be the time to exercise your right to the publisher's money-back guarantee.)

However, for those whom this understanding does not fit, questioning the benefit of the speaching act is an essential element of re-imagining the church and its role in creating people who have a different agenda and desire a different outcome from the current options offered by Christianity.

CHAPTER 14

FEAR OF BEING WRONG

Because so many of us have been schooled in the Lloyd-Jones tradition [13], where preaching is the primary task of the church, it can be daunting to consider a change in preaching tactics and outcomes—it puts at risk the very center of what we think the church is about. Quite honestly, I believe we *should* meet suggestions about such changes with reserved acceptance. I am all for a change in the function of speaching, but I will be the first to say it ought to come with significant consideration; change that comes too easily is often surface change rather than deeply realized re-creation. I also recognize that those who choose to consider these issues will not only need to change the way they preach, but will also eventually come to reconsider the entire enterprise of church in the industrialized world. And that's not always a pleasant process.

That being said, I find there is far too much fear surrounding preaching—fear that if the wrong thing is preached or if the preaching is too weak or too *anything*, then the work of God in the world will suffer. This kind of emphasis on preaching is drawn from a far too limited view of the work of the church and far too heightened understanding of preaching (à la Dr. Lloyd-Jones) [13]. At the same time this fear comes out of a belief that mere mortals have no business presuming to "speak for God" to begin with, and therefore we ought not to insert our own ideas into this most sacred of practices.

Consider this quote from Karl Barth: "What are you doing, you man, with the Word of God upon your lips? Upon what grounds do you assume the role of mediator between heaven and earth? Who has authorized you to take your place there and to generate religious feeling? And to crown all, to do so with results, with success? Who dares, who can preach, knowing what preaching is?" (July 1922, as quoted at *victoryoutreach.org*).

And this from a current Web site:

Preaching is in a class by itself. It is not simply a speech about God. It is rather God himself speaking through the mouth of the preacher. It may seem like foolishness to a world that is skilled in the art of communication, but as Paul wrote in 1 Corinthians 1:21, "God was pleased through the foolishness of what was preached to save those who believe." In Reformed worship preaching the Word is so centrally important because it is a prominent way, perhaps the most prominent way, in which God has chosen to speak to people throughout the ages in order to accomplish his purposes in them. When they reflected on Scripture's call to preach, both Luther and Calvin came to the conclusion that has been so much a part of the Reformed understanding of the place of the sermon in the worship service: If preaching is heralding the good news that God has entrusted to his church, then preaching the Word of God **is** the Word of God.

—Wilbert M. Van Dyk (as quoted on *Pastornet.net*)

For those who take this view of preaching, any suggestion to change it from an act done by a set-apart individual who has been properly trained to handle the Word of God is a frightening prospect. I know pastors who are inclined to try moving away from speaching but who are held back by the fear of opening the floor to comments and ideas from unknown sources. A friend of mine with a divinity degree from an Ivy League seminary told me, "You know, when I hear my former view of preaching stated in such stark terms (as above), it kind of takes the wind out of me. And I'm still not sure I've totally gotten over it."

What I said to him, and what I hope will serve as a way of calming the fears of others who share these concerns, is that speaching is not the ultimate expression of preaching, and preaching is not the ultimate endeavor of the church. In fact, I would argue it's a lesser form of what we are called to do. The Lloyd-Jones/Barthian understanding of preaching is simply an overstatement. It is a perspective held and shared by people with right intentions but what I believe to be misguided conclusions. I urge, implore, beg, and beseech you not to be captivated by this perspective without at least considering that it is just that: a perspective.

Instead know that the invitation to ministry is an invitation to join in the work of God and not to create it; God is at work with or without our sermons. Know that our preaching matters, but it isn't our central contribution; more lives will be changed by the relationships created and lived out in our communities than by what we say in some sermon. Know that we are invited with the empowering of the Holy Spirit to create and reform the way we do everything in the church; that has been the call of ministers from the time of Peter and Paul, and it remains our call today. We cannot fail in the work of God when we seek to be part of the active, re-creative kingdom life.

CHAPTER 15

CENTRALIZED CONTROL

At the heart of the resistance to progressional dialogue as a legitimate method of preaching is the question of control. The speaching act allows for the preacher not only to control the content, but also to apply the sermon to people's lives. In basketball there is an expression for a person who does everything on the court—get the rebound, dribble up court, and shoot. This person is called a ball hog, and no one likes having one on the court.

Is it possible that this kind of phrase could also apply to pastors who do all the studying, all the talking, and even have the gall to think they can apply the messages they create to the lives of other people? In this setting there is little for the hearers to do besides decide if they agree or not. Is it possible that we have, through the practice of speaching, created a culture in churches where agreeability is the necessary posture of our people? And if this is so, does it serve the gospel well?

The problem here is not just the delivery system but the assumption that what people need to know exists in the mind and plans of one person who is often little more than an acquaintance for most of the people in the church. *The Onion* is a satirical newspaper that publishes a combination of fictitious stories and actual advertisements and reviews. With its sharp cultural critique this paper has reached legendary status in some people's minds. Each issue of *The Onion* includes the paper's editorial policy on letters to the editor, which reads—

> *The Onion* neither publishes nor accepts letters from its readers. It is *The Onion's* editorial policy that the readers shall have no voice whatsoever and that *The Onion* newspaper shall be solely a one-way conduit of information. The editorial page is reserved for the exclusive use of the newspaper staff to advance whatever opinion or agenda it sees fit or, in certain cases, for paid advertorials by the business community.
>
> —Passed by a majority of the editorial board, March 17, 1873.

What makes this statement so funny is how outrageous it is when compared with people's expectations of a newspaper. But what makes it sad in the context of a sermon is how close it comes to the truth.

If we truly believe God is involved in the lives of the people of our communities, it seems obvious that we should avoid using a practice that tells them this involvement is determined by others. Why would we call people to a personal connection with God and yet be content to give them generic, universal experiences with the message of faith? I realize it's problematic when one's understanding of the message of God is personal to the point of not being connected to the lives of others, but that's not what I'm advocating. (I make a distinction between "personal" and "individual" because there are many things that are intimate and personal but not individual: memories, sexuality, hopes, and so on.) Christianity is a faith that allows us, even calls us, to have a faith that is deeply meaningful to our lives. We shouldn't be content with speaching that only demeans this message by making it broad and shallow.

This effort to maintain control over a centralized message naturally leads to a centralized understanding of God. At first glance that might sound like a positive outcome. But consider how the church would look today if we'd stuck with one understanding of God throughout all of history. We'd have no way of talking about God as the suffering servant nor any language for liberation theology.

The benefit to living in this time and place is that we have access to an amazing variety of ways to understand, connect with, and grow in God. We can and should benefit from the faith lived by our counterparts in other times and other places. Being part of a global, pluralistic world is a great gift to the church, for our role in ministry is not to push the agenda of our clan but to recognize and join in the life of God wherever we find it. We miss out on that opportunity when we limit our understanding of God to that which is offered by a few "holders of truth." Ironically, even these "experts" are only able to present us with a piece of God. Because each of us has a personal relationship with God, it makes sense that each of us would have a personal understanding of God. Even those of us who like to think we have broad, well-informed concepts of God must recognize that our concepts are filtered through our own experiences of God, as well as the things we were taught, our hopes, and our presuppositions.

During a recent Sunday night we were discussing the story of Jesus healing the leper from the gospel of Mark. Obviously, we don't interact with lepers during the course of our day-to-day activities, but I thought it was consequential for our conversation to have a deeper sense of the issue of leprosy. In putting together my thoughts for the night, I decided that rather than just do research on the issues of leprosy, I'd use some of the sermon time to ask if anyone had ever had contact with a leper. And, of course, someone had. Audrey had visited parts of India where leprosy is a major problem. She was able to talk about the social issues related to leprosy, the religious response of people there, and what our call might be. I did not set this up ahead of time. I knew that even if no one in the room had ever seen or touched a leper, there would be people who knew about it and would be able to share. Audrey's comments helped us all enter a deeper place in the story of Jesus. Her experience added something to our understanding that I couldn't. Even if I had offered research about leprosy, it wouldn't have held the same weight as the life experience of someone who has worked and lived among these people.

There are many pastors who get extremely un-comfortable at the idea of opening the conversation to the comments of other people. Anna, a woman from our church, joined a friend of hers at the friend's church. After the service the two of them began a conversation with the pastor. During the conversation Anna mentioned that we use intentional dialogue during our Tuesday night Bible discussion group to create our sermons and implicate ourselves in the message.

To Anna's surprise the pastor asked, "Who leads these discussions?"

"Well, no one really," Anna replied. "We all add to it, but no one controls it."

Her surprise turned to shock and frustration when the pastor responded by saying, "Discussions that aren't led are dangerous. You never know what people will say."

This fear of uncontrolled conversations about God and the Bible is common in the church. There is not room in this book to discuss fully the number of times our Christian story tells us there is no controlling the activity and work of God, for it seems to me that this is embedded in the entire Bible.

The good news of Jesus was that the kingdom of the God of Israel was present among the people of his day, that God was not limited to the temple practices and was active even among the "unclean" Gentiles. This realization did quite a number on the practices of the early church, practices that were based in large part on synagogue practices and an "old" view of God's activity. The book of Acts records interactions between the church in Jerusalem—the one that held most closely to temple and synagogue practices—and the burgeoning Gentile expressions of faith. It's impossible for us to understand the implications this had for the Jerusalem church and the scandal it must have created. For the leaders of the faith to extend freedom to these untrained, uncircumcised people was a tremendous example of trust in the unpredictable, uncontrollable nature of the Holy Spirit.

Lest we get the impression that the apostles kept a close watch on what was happening in the places where the Holy Spirit was moving in the creation of these Gentile churches, we need to take note of Acts 15:13, 19-29:

> When they finished, James spoke up. "Brothers," he said, "listen to me…It is my judgment, therefore, that we should not make it difficult for the Gentiles who are turning to God. Instead we should write to them, telling them to abstain from food polluted by idols, from sexual immorality, from the meat of strangled animals and from blood. For the law of Moses has been preached in every city from the earliest times and is read in the synagogues on every Sabbath." Then the apostles and elders, with the whole church, decided to choose some of their own men and send them to Antioch with Paul and Barnabas. They chose Judas (called Barsabbas) and Silas, who were leaders among the believers. With them they sent the following letter: The apostles and elders, your brothers, To the Gentile believers in Antioch, Syria and Cilicia: Greetings. We have heard that some went out from us without our authorization and

disturbed you, troubling your minds by what they said. So we all agreed to choose some men and send them to you with our dear friends Barnabas and Paul—men who have risked their lives for the name of our Lord Jesus Christ. Therefore we are sending Judas and Silas to confirm by word of mouth what we are writing. It seemed good to the Holy Spirit and to us not to burden you with anything beyond the following requirements: You are to abstain from food sacrificed to idols, from blood, from the meat of strangled animals and from sexual immorality. You will do well to avoid these things. Farewell.

The promise of the work of the Spirit is that it moves with the freedom of the wind. It blows where it will. Centralizing control in the bowels of the church and its structures robs the Spirit of this freedom.

The Spirit still moves in surprising ways. I've seen it happen over and over in our church. There was a night when a woman who was visiting for the first time raised her hand during the discussion time. She explained that earlier in the gathering she'd felt compelled to turn to a particular psalm. At some point in the sermon I happened to reference this same psalm. She asked if she could read it for us, and of course we agreed she should. The Holy Spirit clearly moved among us in that moment of divine coincidence.

Once we open ourselves to the work of the Spirit, even those things we once thought to be disruptions become fodder for formation. In our community we are fond of saying that when babies cry during our gatherings, this need not be thought of as distracting us from what is being said but understood as a reminder of the importance of listening to one another cry.

We also have a "rule" about cell phones during our worship. We say, "Keep them on; something important might happen." Sure enough, one night the cell phone of Dave, a man in our community, rang in the middle of the sermon, and he answered it. People snickered a bit because of the volume of his conversation. I kept talking, but I noticed Dave was quite disturbed by the content of the phone call. He got up to continue his conversation away from the gathering space, and after my part of the sermon I saw him in the lobby. It turned out his father had suffered a major heart attack and was being rushed to the hospital. When he finished the call, we went back to the gathering and told everyone what was happening. We quickly surrounded Dave and prayed for his father.

The content of the sermon that night included stories of Jesus healing the sick. We could have talked about those stories all night and never reached the point of living it the way we did when we were drawn into Dave's pain and his father's suffering. If we'd had the attitude that a cell phone ringing during our worship gathering was a distraction from the important things of God, we would have missed the chance to do the things of God.

There is something positive about telling people they need not set aside their everyday lives to interact with the things of God. The attitude of "Listen to me because this is the most important thing you will hear today" may create more centralized control, but it's not good for the good news.

CHAPTER 16

FEAR OF HERESY

At the heart of this clinging to control is a genuine desire to protect the community from heresy. Yet I believe progressional preaching is one of the best ways to do exactly that. Throughout the centuries the church has used two primary tools to identify and prevent heresy: the work of the Holy Spirit and the communion of saints. Speaching is a shift from this practice. When a few people are able to control the message of the community, and the people have no way to speak into that power, the community is in danger.

Progressional preaching forces pastors to move beyond reductionistic thinking. If a speaker is allowed to speak with the authority of the church and offer explanations and applications on issues of life and faith, those explanations and applications must be open to question, to clarification, to expansion. Without this kind of input and response a pastor can easily slip into a pattern of one-size-fits-all theology that serves no one.

For many pastors, statements of faith set the boundaries for the sermon. The problem is that statements of faith usually serve to keep people away from the church more than they draw them in. That's because they're usually statements about what this church or denomination believes, and the implicit message is that anyone who walks through the door needs to believe these things as well. The statement is a closed conversation, one that has already taken place and has no room for the voice of someone new.

For pastors who want their preaching to engage people in the entire life of the community, these statements tend to work against that end. Statements of faith never state *everything* a person or church believes; they can only offer what they believe on particular topics. In addition, they can't possibly include *every* topic, so they tend to focus on the topics where they differ from the beliefs or doctrines of other churches. In other words, the statements aren't full expressions of what a community believes. When people in the church are required to stay within those parameters, they are less likely to engage. And when they do engage, they rarely want to fight the battles that seemed so important to the framers of that set of statements.

So what is a church to hold to if it isn't a classic statement of faith? I suggest holding to all the church has held to throughout its history. If a belief is in harmony with historical Christianity, then it should be seen as a valid position. This means people will often hold contradictory positions, but that's a good thing.

Most of the time my community won't allow me to get away with simple conclusions or sloppy theology. Just knowing that those listening to me will have a chance to ask questions, seek clarification, or expand on what I've said makes me a more thoughtful preacher. It also makes us a more thoughtful community.

One night I was in the midst of going on and on about how Jesus was using apocalyptic language and the role that kind of language played in the first century. But instead of saying "apocalyptic," I kept saying "Armageddon." I noticed that each time I said it, Dan, a young man in our community who is currently in seminary and who was sitting not three feet from me, would smile. I couldn't figure out why. I'd even wanted to put some context around the word *apocalypse* by mentioning the movie *Apocalypse Now*, but I couldn't figure out the name of the movie in my head, and I sort of stumbled over that part.

I think those who realized what I'd done were embarrassed for me, as no one said a thing about it during the sermon discussion. So it wasn't until the next week when Dan finally told me why he'd been smiling that I realized my mistake. I mentioned this exchange during the sermon and reminded everyone that this interaction requires their participation and protection. This time it had been a simple mix-up of my words, but I needed them to know they have not only the chance, but also the responsibility to call me out when I say something they know to be wrong.

Progressional preaching creates freedom in the preacher and the community. There is relief in knowing that the pastor's voice is not the only one people will hear on important issues of faith. For me knowing others are going to interact with the sermon functions like the "undo" button on my computer. I can type with confidence, knowing I can erase what I've written. Or if I make a mistake and erase something I wanted to keep, I can get it back with a few clicks of my mouse. This freedom doesn't give me permission to be lax in my preparation and preaching; rather it allows me to explore ideas and share not only what I am certain of, but also those things I'm in the midst of pondering myself. Knowing others will add to the conversation lets me talk about and live out my faith in a much more honest and vulnerable way. Certainly we need to tread somewhat carefully to ensure we don't create a sense that no one knows anything and everything is up for grabs. But with the current state of the church after decades of speaching, I think we have plenty of room to explore this freedom.

One night after our worship gathering I went to a nearby church to speak at their evening service. As I drove there, I became anxious about how different this preaching experience was going to be. Since no one would have the chance to respond to the sermon, I had to be sure everything was just right: If someone had the ability to correct me or add to what I was saying, I would never know it. The difference between the freedom I felt in our setting and the concern I had going into that speaching setting was palpable.

CHAPTER 17

TRUTH

I realize many pastors—and many Christians, for that matter—grow exceedingly nervous at the idea of introducing uncertainty and fluidity to conversations about God and faith. So many Christians feel the church is under attack by a culture of relativism that they're hesitant to let any ambiguity trickle into their theology. They feel a strong call to be protectors of the truth. This sense of duty to guard the truth holds them back from entering into progressional dialogue.

Any conversation around the issue of truth benefits from a clarification of terms. When we talk about truth, we're really considering two concepts: reality (the way things are) and truth (a person's perspective of that reality). One of the problems with the use of the word *truth* is the adjectives people use with it: absolute, total, unquestioned, complete. These adjectives don't bolster truth; they redefine it. If what people mean when they use these qualifiers is that their view is the only view, then that isn't truth—at least by my definition. It's dogma, and it's rarely useful.

No one has access to all reality in such a way that he can conclusively call his experience and understanding *the* truth. We all operate out of our own contexts; we all understand the world in certain terms and with particular categories that are important, meaningful, and sufficient. We benefit when we are in contact with others who help us develop new categories. No perspective of reality matters unless it matters to someone. So we are helped when we understand the reasons why something matters to another person. This is how we grow, learn, and develop.

The goal of truth-seeking ought to be more than finding support for the perspective I already haveDave, but also to broaden and deepen my perspective of the world by figuring out how the perspective of another dovetails into or corrects my own. This all becomes quite important when trying to move from speaching to progressional dialogue. If we think the job of the preacher is to make truth claims that secure the beliefs people already have or to present truth claims to non-truth holders so they will accept them, we have a problem. Because of the assumed power of the preacher, our words are not understood as truth meant to be viewed as one perspective of reality, but as The Truth that isn't touched by the truths of others, certainly not the truths of those listening to the sermon. We shut down the chance for a person's perspective to be taken seriously.

I'm not suggesting a weak belief system but one that recognizes the reality of our perceptions. What I know to be true is not negated by others knowing more or other things. Truth is progressive, not regressive or zero sum. When someone knows something to be true, it doesn't remove the legitimacy of other truths but adds to it. We may not agree with the conclusions people draw, but we're better when we're moved to additional ways of seeing the world.

There are those who say the church has a responsibility to promote a Christian worldview. But pastors alone do not constitute the church. We don't own the Christian worldview, and we shouldn't be the only ones allowed to contribute to the ways in which that worldview is shaped. The beauty of progressional dialogue is that it returns the ownership of the Christian perspective to the body of Christ, the people who truly are the church.

It is my understanding of the story of faith that people are called to be full participants in ministry and have been since the very beginning. Jesus called his followers into lives lived in community (John 13). Paul used metaphor after metaphor to help the church understand their interdependence (1 Corinthians 12). Neither of them excluded the ignorant or the uneducated from involvement in the community. In fact, it was often the outsider, the unexpected voice, who drew the attention of the Messiah.

The Holy Spirit has always been the sign that God's presence was upon someone, setting him apart for a holy purpose (see Judges 6:34; 1 Samuel 16:13; Ezekiel 11:5). In the Old Testament the prophet Isaiah said, "The Spirit of the Sovereign Lord is on me, because the Lord has anointed me to proclaim good news to the poor" (Isaiah 61:1). Jesus' life was marked by the presence and power of the Spirit of God. But on the day of Pentecost the followers of Jesus were in the upper room together, and the Holy Spirit fell on all of them (Acts 2). This was more than just a strange happening; it was a sign that the Spirit, once upon only a select few, was now upon them all.

The people of God, in communion with the Bible and the Holy Spirit, have the truth of God within them. That is, the story of God helps us interpret the reality with which we interact. The Holy Spirit guides this interaction and interpretation. Every person has experience, understanding, and perspective; there is no one who is totally devoid of truth.

We have a person in our community who is in the midst of a profound struggle with sexuality and gender. Chris's issues are well-known in our community and dealt with in an honest, open, and compassionate way. As a regular part of our Sunday gatherings, Kathryn, a woman in our community, leads us in prayer. These prayers often involve people reading a prayer or demonstrating a posture for prayer. One evening Kathryn asked Chris to do one of the readings. It was a subtle gesture on Kathryn's part, one that told our community not that there is nothing wrong in Chris's life and therefore she gets to lead us in prayer, but that we recognize there *is* something wrong in Chris's life—and she still gets to lead us in prayer. If we are going to grapple with what it means to be the church, we need to be willing to incorporate the truth of Chris's life, along with the truths of Kathryn's and Doug's and Jimmy's lives.

CHAPTER 18

THE POWER OF CONTROL

In the summer of 2004 Jake, one of the young men in our community, joined the army. He'd served as a mentor to our son Taylor and was quite close to our family, so we arranged our family vacation around attending his graduation from basic training at Fort Leonard Wood in Missouri. I'd never been to anything quite like this graduation. We took a tour of the facility and watched groups of soldiers in the midst of their training on that hot summer day—running and doing calisthenics in pits filled with crushed tires. We watched as these young women and men were reshaped into fighting soldiers.

I've never had a desire to join the military and have deep concerns about the practice of training people to be "killing machines." But during the graduation we were in an auditorium with about 300 people—100 graduating soldiers and their families. It was obvious to me that a number of the graduates were from military families. Here I found myself in a community with strong feelings about national service in the military; and before I knew it, I found myself being drawn in to their emotions and experiences.

Looking into the eyes of these people—many of whom were very young or not what I would consider to be fighting material—I couldn't help but think about what I knew they knew—that in a matter of months nearly all of them would face combat in Iraq or Afghanistan. I'm not a fan of country music and have concerns about the tough-guy Americana music that has surrounded the war on terror. But while I was sitting in the presence of those new soldiers, watching a slideshow of images portraying soldiers in combat and the attacks on the World Trade Center towers and Pentagon on September 11, 2001, listening to a song about the eagle flying as our American soldiers rain down vengeance on the enemies of freedom, I was overwhelmed, and it all seemed to make sense. I couldn't fight back the tears or the thoughts that what Jake was doing was an honorable thing.

The centerpiece of the ceremony was the recitation of "The Soldier's Creed." To hear the young men and women say these words with urgency, seriousness, and passion almost did me in:

> I am an American soldier.
> I am a warrior and a member of a team. I serve the people of the United States and live the Army values.
> I will always place the mission first.
> I will never accept defeat.
> I will never quit.
> I will never leave a fallen comrade.
> I am disciplined, physically and mentally tough, trained and proficient in my warrior tasks and drills.

I always maintain my arms, my equipment, and myself.

I am an expert and I am a professional.

I stand ready to deploy, engage, and destroy the enemies of the United States of America in close combat.

I am a guardian of freedom and the American way of life.

I am an American soldier.

—*www.army.mil/thewayahead/creed.html*

Normally, the language of this creed would really rub me the wrong way, especially hearing it from the mouth of a young man I know to be a person of love and compassion. But it didn't seem a bit odd to me in that room. Instead it seemed fitting and honorable. My concerns and discomfort seemed to be swallowed up in this atmosphere. I found myself feeling like I understood everything they understood.

But when we were driving home, I started to think more about our time there and why that environment would cause me to have such a different feeling about these issues. I remember thinking, *It all made sense when I was there, but now I'm not so sure if all of that was a good idea.*

My thoughts then turned to how people have similar experiences in church. The odd things we do—the speaches, the music, the liturgy—all make sense in the environments we create. The problem comes when the same people drive home and reenter a life where none of these forms are present. The switch is so evident, it can be destabilizing. Perhaps that's why we seek to keep control and structure in our collective experiences of faith and worship rather than consider ways to make the differences between life "out there" and life "in here" a little less dramatic.

Controlling the content of what is said about God certainly has its appeal. It allows us to mold communities of people who think certain ways and behave in certain ways. It creates a kind of dependence on the pastor as the only person who can chart the course of the community. It takes away the threat of instability that comes when people question the message. But the church isn't the military. It isn't meant to be a place where we train soldiers for battle and send them out with infallible marching orders. It's meant to be the place where we encounter God together and figure out how to live in the kingdom life to which we are called.

CHAPTER 19

PASTORAL AUTHORITY

I truly believe most of us end up clinging to control not out of some ego-driven sense of pride or hubris but out of a deep belief that it's what we're called to do. The idea that we can and should see preaching as a community act goes against the too-common idea that the preacher is the preacher because she's been chosen by God to be the authoritative spokesperson on the things of God. This understanding hurts both the pastor and the community.

Preaching isn't a choice for most pastors. It's part of the larger call to ministry that leads most of us to the pastorate in the first place. We don't want to be people who are set apart from the Christian community; we want to be people who are living lives of faithfulness to God and service to people. Most of us never wanted to be the spokespersons for all of faith. Not only do we not want to, but we also know we can't fulfill this.

There is a sense in many churches that the pastor is sort of the resident "holy one," or at least holier than average. The fact that we have to stand up in front of everyone and tell them the way things are turns up the pressure for us to live up to what we're saying. So the pastor had better practice what he preaches. This gives the pastor little permission for growth and maturation, little space to move further into life in the way of Jesus, because he was supposed to be there all along. At the same time the pastor is supposed to bear all the burden of having something fresh to share each week. This pressure begins to erode the soul of the preacher like waves on rock.

The effect of water on rock is amazing. It's hard to believe that sand on a beach is the result of years of relentless waves pulverizing rock into fine powder. Even more amazing to me are rock shelves. If you've ever seen one, you know that when you look at the sections of rock that sit in the water, they look perfectly normal. But when you explore the rock from under the water, you discover that water has crept behind the rock for years and eroded it away from below. What looks like a solid rock cliff is actually only inches thick. When I see one of these, I'm tempted to stand on it, but because there is little left below the surface, this seemingly indestructible rock could not bear the weight of my body. It's only a matter of time before the rock fully gives way.

There's only so much a person can take of being the lone voice of faith. I recall a conversation at a pastors' event where preachers of large and successful churches were asked to share how they keep their own lives fresh and their faiths vital. The number of pastors who didn't find encouragement and strength in their own churches shocked me. More often than not church ministry was seen as a stress that needed to be addressed. Something is tragically amiss when the life-giving gospel becomes hazardous to the lives of the people most engaged in it.

Imagine what our churches would be like if the entire community felt called to practice what they preach. Imagine how it would feel to pastor a church where the people understood themselves to be ministers. Imagine if, rather than holding the pastor to a standard higher than that to which they hold themselves, our communities believed themselves to carry some of the holiness they attribute to the pastor. Some will argue that Paul's admonition to Timothy should be seen as a call for pastors to be held to a higher standard: "Here is a trustworthy saying: Whoever aspires to be an overseer desires a noble task. Now the overseer is to be above reproach, faithful to his wife, temperate, self controlled, respectable, hospitable, able to teach, not given to drunkenness, not violent but gentle, not quarrelsome, not a lover of money" (1 Timothy 3:1-3). But who would suggest that Paul believed this was not also the expectation for the people of the church?

Speaching leaves pastors with little choice but to remain seated in the "expert" chair, whether we like being there or not. Progressional preaching allows us to move back into a rightful place of walking with our brothers and sisters, of being open to the formative work of God in our own hearts and lives, of being people of God first and pastors second.

CHAPTER 20

TRANSMITTING THE MESSAGE

Many of us have become so comfortable with the concept of the stranger speaching to the stranger that we pay little attention to the ways interpersonal communication actually works. We've traded our understanding of basic human relationships for formulas best suited to classroom instruction. While these formulas and methods work just fine for transferring information from one person to another, they fall dramatically short in nurturing the souls of human beings.

So often when I read books or attend seminars on preaching, they invariably touch on the subject of how to increase the "transfer integrity" of the message. Pastors are encouraged to make adjustments to help people retain an increased percentage of what is being said in the sermon, based on the idea that people remember 10 percent of what they hear, 50 percent of what they hear and see, and 90 percent of what they hear, see, and do. So speakers are encouraged to use visual and audio aids such as movie clips or bits of popular songs to add impact to their speaches. They might be encouraged to make up worksheets for the congregation to use at home or in their small groups to help the message sink in.

But these tactics can often backfire by actually subverting the very relationship they are intended to forge. My friend John Musik is the pastor of a church called Bluer in Minneapolis. John told me a story that serves as a great example of the ways in which our efforts to heighten transmission can get in the way of our actual mission:

> We have gone through several amalgamations in our struggle to find Bluer's identity and refine our purpose. One of our versions was what we called "Big Bluer." Big Bluer met in an 800-seat converted movie theater in a suburb of Minneapolis. We packed the place with enough equipment and technology to do whatever our imaginations could come up with. And stopping short of shooting me out of a cannon, we did some great stuff.
>
> Big Bluer had a large theatrical stage that rose three-and-a-half feet off the floor and was set back twelve feet from the front row of seating. Overhead we had an expansive network of catwalks from which hung a monster sound system, a dozen intelligent lighting fixtures that would shine colored lights and graphics wherever we programmed them to, and four large Fresnel Lights that flooded the stage.
>
> Our services began with a worship performance that employed video graphics projected on a 24-foot-high screen and smoke machines. Then it was time for me to speak. My image was also projected onto the screen, and for the cameras to clearly pick me up, the

tech guys would blast the Fresnel lights at me. They were so bright they literally blinded me from seeing the audience. Thankfully, I could see to the edge of the stage so I didn't walk off the edge, but I could see no further.

In this snow-blind state, I had to imagine where people were in order to make "eye contact" with the congregation. To keep things lively I paced back and forth, gestured dramatically, and stopped periodically to address certain portions of the theater. The only problem was that there were often large sections of chairs where nobody was sitting. So there I would be, making an impassioned appeal to expanses of empty chairs! I'm sure the people were thinking to themselves, *Who on earth is he talking to? There's nobody over there.*

I was king in the story of the Emperor's New Clothes, my folly being revealed to all. Here I was trying to connect with people and be authentic, and I couldn't even see them.

Many may argue these types of additions help people retain what they hear, and what could be wrong with that? But to me this entire notion is based on the wrong premise. It seems to suggest lives lived in greater harmony with God will come if people simply retain more of what we're telling them. It's as though we believe the problem is people not hearing or remembering what we've said. I believe Christianity suffers not because people don't know the message but because people hear the message and reject it.

We would never approach another kind of relationship with the rules we apply to the speacher/hearer relationship. I speak with my wife nearly every day. Because we communicate with each other, we both are shaped by these interactions. If she were simply to listen to me every day and not have the opportunity to give her take on things, our marriage would not be a healthy one for either of us. I guess I could talk to my wife and then let her know that she should talk with her friends about what I've said or that she can come to me if she needs any clarification. But somehow I don't think that would fly. I'd be accused—and rightly so—of having significant power issues. In the same way, being part of a church for 12 years and hearing the pastor's thoughts some 600 times but never having the pastor hear yours is a dangerous imbalance of power.

We need a new way of being, a new reality to invite people into, and we cannot simply focus on reducing transmission loss. Speaching's failures are not addressed by getting people more engaged in our pastoral agenda. We need to connect our agendas with God's agenda and be implicated by what we discover.

SECTION FIVE
WHY WE NEED TO CHANGE

CHAPTER 21

THE PRIESTHOOD OF ALL BELIEVERS

While I do hold that people are gifted, prepared, and prompted by God for the teaching and benefit of the community of faith, I don't think those who are so gifted are specially ordained to lead a community to the exclusion of all others. If that sounds odd to you, I'd ask you to consider the biblical notion of the priesthood of all believers in 1 Peter 2:9.

The idea that all believers are included in the "royal priesthood" Peter speaks of was crucial to the early church. But over the centuries it got lost in the structure and ceremony of church life. When the Reformation took place, the language of the priesthood of all believers once again took hold but very slowly—so slowly that we still seem unsure of its implications for the church.

I'd like to suggest one: A belief in the priesthood of all believers compels us to reconsider our ideas about speaching and pastoral authority. Preaching is the act of people being led more deeply in to the story of God. This was never meant to take place through the act of speech giving. Even in the rare instances in the Bible when speeches are made, they fit into the context of a community that is in near-constant dialogue. In fact, a great deal of the spiritual formation that happens to people in the Bible takes place outside of any sort of "church" environment. People in the Bible meet God when they are walking to a neighboring village, when they are talking with unlikely messengers, when they are in the midst of crisis. The idea, then, that only a trained professional can speak about God with any kind of authority goes against nearly everything we find in Scripture.

In truth the idea that a person needs to be specifically educated to understand the things of God is little more than Western conceit. We are unique in our belief that education leads to superiority, that the preliterate or illiterate are somehow less qualified to be vessels of God in the world. There was a time when churches believed that the pastor should be the sole speaker for God because he was among the few who could read, as though the only important knowledge of God is the kind that comes from reading. We still, too often, behave in a way that suggests we believe the only legitimate means to understanding or experiencing God is education. Obviously, there are benefits to having a pastor with some theological education, but what if we thought of that education as a gift the pastor brings to the community, one that melds with the gifts and life experiences of others to create a rich, multifaceted community of faith? Imagine the response if people in our churches believed their gifts, ideas, and experiences were as inspired by God as those of the preacher.

CHAPTER 22

TRUSTING THE PEOPLE

It's hard for those of us living on the presentation side of speaching to know what it does in the lives of the recipients. When competent, educated, well-informed people are put in the position of listening to someone give one-way presentations on issues of God week in and week out, they have a choice to make: Will they stand for it or not? There are many who have chosen not to take it any longer.

A friend of mine who serves on the staff of a large, successful church told me about a conversation he had with his senior pastor. My friend wanted to know why a certain man in their church did not attend even though his children were regulars in the youth ministry. To my friend's surprise the senior pastor mentioned that the father was a wealthy, powerful man and said, "Powerful men don't come to places where other men tell them how to live their lives." The shock for my friend was not only that the pastor knew this and seemed comfortable with it, but also that the pastor didn't act as though he needed to make any adjustments in his preaching style as a result.

I believe this sentiment is present even among people who are not financially wealthy or powerful; there are many people who aren't interested in being part of meetings where strangers use speaches to tell them how to live. The very people we are trying to engage with the life-changing, implicatory gospel are the ones who are creating new thinking and technology, teaching their children, interacting in classrooms and on blogs, giving advice to friends, talking in coffee shops, answering questionnaires from pollsters, reading and writing books, watching and creating brilliant television shows and movies, and sorting through thousands of messages communicated to them each day. Yet at church these same people are told that the important things of God reside in the mind of the speech maker alone. It's a wonder *anyone* puts up with it.

CHAPTER 23

THE ROLE OF THE PASTOR

Progressional dialogue significantly changes the relationship between the pastor and the congregation. And that's a good thing. Too often the role of the pastor is reduced to being someone who knows a lot about something obscure (in our case, the Bible and theology) but doesn't do much outside of that.

One night during the most recent summer Olympics, I found myself awake well past my bedtime and watching the trampoline competition. I couldn't drag myself away. I was enthralled with these people who were performing a sport that, until that night, I had no idea *was* a sport. Even though I knew nothing about competitive trampoline jumping, the commentators brought it to life for me. They knew everything about the sport—the intricacies of the jumps, the strengths of the athletes, the strategies needed to win, the complexities of the scoring.

I started wondering about these commentators: Who are they? What do they do when there are no Olympics? How did they learn all this stuff? What good is this information when they aren't commentating? Then it struck me that there are occasional Sunday nights when I feel like I'm little more than an expert commentator. I'm the guy who knows things about the Bible and Christian faith, things that help me see what is going on in a biblical passage that other people wouldn't even notice. What if the people in my church view me the same way I view these commentators? What if they think of me as a guy who knows enough about the Bible to make it accessible and interesting for them, but apart from that I'm not really all that useful?

Not only do I want to believe I play a more significant role in my community than just being the guy who knows about the Bible, but the community also deserves more from me. I watched the trampoline competition for way too long, but even the excellent commentary couldn't turn me into an Olympic jumper. I could rattle off everything there is to know about being a competitive trampoliner, but that's not the same as being a jumper. I need more than an expert commentator to help me rearrange my life in such a way that I become an Olympic athlete. I need relationships with coaches and other jumpers who help me immerse myself in this new commitment.

The role of a progressional preacher is so much more than the role of the expert. Consider these words to Timothy, "You then, my son, be strong in the grace that is in Christ Jesus. And the things you have heard me say in the presence of many witnesses entrust to reliable people who will also be qualified to teach others" (2 Timothy 2:1-2). Those are valuable words to progressional preachers, for we are the conduits that allow the people of the church to interact with, learn from, and be remade by the whole community of faith.

CHAPTER 24

PROPHETIC FUNCTION

I am increasingly convinced that we would do well to expand our understanding of Jesus to include his role as a prophet on a prophet's task. A prophet is one who calls the people of faith to live the dreams and aspirations of God in particular ways. Prophetic communities are those that allow others to join in the activity of God in their day. This is a different function from being communities where people are taught to believe certain things or to maintain structures designed in and for other times and places. Prophetic communities are called to a life that is particular to the here and now.

Jesus, it seems to me, was concerned with life lived in faith, and he used prophetic words and actions to show and bring about that life: welcoming little children, putting his hands on the "unclean," talking with and listening to the outsider, forgiving sin, and putting the kingdom call in the hands of the "nonordained" of his day. One could argue that these were strategic tactics Jesus used to connect with people as they listened to him. But I don't think Jesus was being strategic. He was being prophetic. We're in trouble when we can't distinguish the two or worse yet when we leave out the prophetic mission and are left only with the strategic.

We ought to live in ways that are prophetic—calling people to new ways of living by living with them differently. We ought to understand churches as being more like prophetic communities than Christian teaching sites. The churches described in the New Testament had this sense. They were alternative and contemporary. In other words, they were distinct from the world they lived in. They were not generically alternative, with every church looking and acting the same. So the church in Ephesus had a different feel to it than the church in Corinth. They had different challenges, different strengths, different missions. What they shared was their desire to be alternatives to other ways of ordering the world. This being the case, the role of preaching in prophetic communities ought to be a practice that builds prophetic life, an alternative way.

Progressional preaching is an act that challenges social and cultural norms. People have become used to churches supplying them with spiritual life assistance, where they sit as consumers. The act of preaching ought to call us to something different. When we seek to live in new ways that remove the power structures that have kept people from connecting with faith, we are being prophetic, not hip. Moving the power from the speaker to the audience is not simply a ploy to be experiential—it's an attempt to live into the new things of God.

SECTION SIX
HOW TO MAKE THE MOVE

CHAPTER 25

NEW OUTCOMES

The whole point of preaching is to help people grow in their understanding of God and how we are to live as God's people and to empower the church to live out God's mission. Any conversation about preaching must involve a sense of how our sermons accomplish these purposes. My contention is that speaching, while perhaps a reasonable way to deliver a broad message to a broad group of people, is not a sustainable means for building Christian communities who seek to live in harmony with God, each other, and the world. I am not suggesting a move to progressional preaching as the sole means to this end—it will take a comprehensive approach—but I do believe that only when we change our ideas about speaching will we change the ways our communities articulate, express, and embody the hopeful message of God.

One of the hurdles we need to get over to think about the outcomes of our preaching is the idea that it's primarily an act of evangelism, which puts us in a place of seeking essentially the same outcome year after year, just in different people. I suggest we move toward new outcomes, even in the same people. While these ought not be in conflict with one another, let me be clear that this conversation is not driven by the need to extend a product to a growing and untapped market. This is a conversation about the kind of people the church is comprised of and the kind of lives we desire to lead.

That in itself has implications for outreach; people who aren't interested in the twentieth-century, North American version of Christianity are not rejecting us because they're ignorant of our message but because they're uninterested in the kind of life we are propagating. Our problem is not one of marketing but of an inferior product. Whether we preach for evangelism, preach for discipleship, or preach for both, we cannot ignore the indications that speaching is failing to accomplish much of anything.

There is a sense in which speaking is a creative act. God spoke—and there was light. Speaking is a way in which people become involved in a situation; the essence of humanity is participation. We pastors understand this, and many churches have worked very hard to encourage people to participate in worship, usually through music or drama or dance. It really isn't a big leap to apply this same understanding of the importance of participation to the preaching act.

This isn't just an effort to make the church experience feel more inclusive or interactive. It isn't a cheap ploy meant to make the church feel fun or unique. I truly believe progressional dialogue is necessary to move people into fuller, richer lives of faith. People's lives are not changed by the information they get. Lives are changed by new situations, new practices, and new ways of experiencing the world. This kind of change can't be delivered from a distance. It's not brought about by well-crafted words or flashy technology. This new life is brought about by the intentional placement of life on life. We want to hear of real life change happening in others' lives so we know it's possible. But these stories can't be the packaged, practiced, anecdotal versions so often intended to make speaching feel more personal. These stories must be accessed through lives that are lived together week after week after week.

It's not my place to tell other pastors and other communities what it will look like for them to live in the kingdom of God. In other words, I'm not going to write out a list of desired outcomes for all churches in all contexts. Even in my church the specifics of who we are and how we live change as we change—we've grown, we've moved, we've aged, and these factors all impact the kind of people we believe ourselves to be and how we see ourselves working in the world. What I *can* give you is a sense of my imaginings for the kinds of churches we can build when we are open to re-creating ourselves and rethinking the ways we preach. I hope these will be stepping-off points for imaginings of your own.

I imagine churches where life is lived with open-eyed optimism. Many people believe we live in the greatest time in history, and the church can and should be part of all that is good and right in the world. Doing so takes a kind of optimism that understands the reality of the world—which isn't always pretty—but sees the hope of God living and active in all of the world. This positivism is reconstructive. It moves beyond critiquing culture and toward constructive change. The intent is not to cultivate a Christian subculture in which we maintain a separateness from the "godless" culture around us but to be useful to the world through new ways of being Christian and new kinds of faith communities. Figuring out how to do this takes the vision and dreaming of all members of the community, not just the pastors.

I imagine churches that live life in rhythm with God. I understand the gospel in terms of Jesus' radical and expansive message of the kingdom of God. Christianity involves much more than a belief in Jesus and an allegiance to a particular expression of faith or dogma. It involves a desire for the good news of Jesus to be truly good news for the people of the world right now. It's not just a promise of a world to come but the promise that is visible in the world today. My friend Mark Scandrette, of re/IMAGINE in San Francisco, articulated this way of living in an e-mail he wrote to me:

> When Jesus described the kingdom of God, he told stories of life. He offered not logical proofs or sterile dogma but demonstration and an invitation to come and walk in a new way. The kingdom of God is about the pursuit of everyday spirituality, about people helping each other live lives that are holistic, integrative, and faithful to the way of Jesus.

> The kingdom of God is a generative people who believe that a more beautiful and sustainable way of life is possible. We explore what it means to be human and spiritual amid the complexities of contemporary society. We live in the creative tension

between thinking well and living well. It is about everything because everything matters. This is about people captured by a story of redemption that impacts every dimension of life. We seek a spirituality that is earthy, human, thoughtful, connected, and aware.

Living this way cannot happen when we think of our faith in individual terms. It can only come when we understand ourselves to be people in community—both with our fellow Christians and with our fellow human beings. It's a life implicated by the power of the good news.

I imagine churches living in partnership with all who are doing the work of God in the world. Our competition is not others who are seeking to do God's work but those who are seeking to destroy it. The way of Jesus is not owned fully by any church expression. So often our church life is one based on fear—fear of the outsider, fear of the unorthodox or unusual, fear of the new or unproven, fear of the traditional and staid. As a result we shut down the re-creative spirit of God. I imagine churches who don't set out to be anti-anything but who instead long to offer the best of what they have experienced in their faith to help us all move forward in the way of Jesus.

I imagine churches that recognize we live in a particular time in history. We have the benefit of those who have gone before us, those around the world (to whom we now have unprecedented access), and those who will follow us and learn from our way of faith. We have the benefit of being the church both in a diverse world and in particular places and neighborhoods, a dichotomy that challenges us to live our faith in ways never dreamed of by those who came before us. The story of who we are in God did not begin with us nor will it end with us. Applying God's Word to our lives might be helpful for the moment, but it does little to advance the story. It does little to make us into people who can look at the world around us and say, "How are we to live God's story in this place and time?"

I imagine churches that believe deep friendships change people. Jesus welcomed the original disciples into warm friendship with himself and one another. Throughout the centuries the church has been at its best when it's been an extension of this friendship and has taken seriously Jesus' invitation to be his friend and friends to one another (John 15:15). When we're not careful, our churches can lose the spirit of true hospitality and friendship that are the core of life-changing relationships. When I speak of hospitality, I don't mean a lunch-in-the-church-basement kind of hospitality. I mean something that takes the kindness and generosity of those meals and adds a new level of vulnerability. This vulnerability is a step beyond accountability. Accountability assumes a person will do her own work as she seeks to live a Christian life while others will do what they can to keep her on track. Vulnerability is a call beyond merely asking others to hold us to living in the way of Jesus—it's inviting them to participate in our efforts to do so. Vulnerability allows those around us to participate in our redemption. This kind of friendship isn't just a nicety; it's a necessity if we are to be people of change. And speaching will not get us there for the simple reason that its assumptions about expertise and authority don't allow for vulnerability.

I imagine churches that seek to be full theological communities. This involves more than changing the methods or structures of church life. It means a new vision of what the church can be. The church can be the place where we move from "cover versions" of the faith of previous generations to living, breathing theological communities who articulate and generate new understandings of God, life, and faith. This can only happen when the process is taken seriously, where people are consciously and consistently invited into conversations about the things of God. Long gone are the days when a select few would go to a hallowed place to learn theology and then return and apply it to the waiting masses. Our churches are stronger and better when the *people* are the church and the community is fully engaged in all matters of faith.

I imagine churches that see themselves as being for both the new convert and the experienced Christian. This kind of life asks us to expand our understanding of conversion. Rather than seeing it as a one-time event, we ought to think of conversion as a lifelong process, one in which all of us are engaged all the time. This new understanding allows us not only to believe the things of Christianity, but also to contextualize, create, and articulate living expressions of faith in the world. It frees us to be people who are constantly re-imagining the kingdom and what it can look like.

I imagine churches that see themselves as more than the context for speaching. The idea that church is a once-a-week event dismantles everything the gospel calls us to be about. When the worship event centers on speaching, the message to the people is clear: The focus of our life together is this 20-minute segment; the rest is gravy. But when preaching becomes an act of community formation, there is an implicit invitation for participation in the full life of the community. It's a clear signal that we are about more than teaching, telling, and learning about God. We are about living in the story of God in all times and in all places.

CHAPTER 26

A DEEP ECCLESIOLOGY

There are multiple ways of connecting people to the dialogue that go far beyond a question-and-answer format. While some of them will involve a long process of rethinking many of our assumptions about church and preaching, we don't need to have everything in place before making a change. I know of a church where the pastor sends the sermon to a select group of people the Thursday before the worship service so they can read it and e-mail their responses. At another church small group leaders are sent the sermon topic and ideas for discussion to use with their small groups before the sermon. Still another church holds an open discussion in the fellowship lounge for an hour after the service. I know of a church where they are having people listen to the sermon with the intention of giving feedback when it is over. None of these ideas is earth-shattering in its originality or cleverness. But each one is life-changing for the people taking part in the life of their church in a new way.

I was leading a seminar in London where we discussed this notion of progressional dialogue preaching. Simon Johnston, the pastor of a church in central London called Head Space, was there. A few weeks later Simon sent me an instant message to tell me he'd given progressional preaching a shot the Sunday following the seminar. Here's what he told me:

> The idea of doing a collective sermon seemed interesting to me, so we gave it a try. Temptation was our theme, and I figured the community knew about as much as me on the subject matter for the day. I started by giving some thoughts and then drew an imaginary line up the middle of the congregation, read the story of Joseph and Potiphar's wife from [Genesis] 39 to one side and David and Bathsheba from 2 Samuel 11 to the other side. Both sides got to work on how each of these guys dealt with temptation in different ways with very different outcomes. I asked both sides to give feedback on any possible lessons, which they did. As someone with a roving mic made their way through the community, listening to thoughts, feelings, and other feedback, I made notes. After this I gave them 10 minutes to talk with each other and carry on their conversations as I pulled together their feedback and constructed a "sermon" from it. Needless to say, many e-mailed the following day and expressed appreciation at being involved in the sermon.

Simon created a sermon from the insights and leadings of the people of his community and preached it back to them. There are few better expressions of interactive preaching than this. We need to create environments where having people contribute is not an interruption to what we are doing but an addition to who we are becoming.

As I've mentioned, preaching is a practice that shapes us, but it isn't the point of ministry. So we must consider not only the content of our sermons, but also how the practice of preaching interacts with who we are seeking to become. There is a need to create entire settings where people listen to one another and learn from those who don't normally share. This will play out in the ways we gather for our worship, the role of the pastor, the structures of our organization, every area of our churches.

At Solomon's Porch our interactive preaching style works because we've tried to create a system that is open. One Sunday I did a quick count and realized there were nine people who led our community in some way, and that didn't include the many musicians and people sharing parts of their stories or contributing to the sermon. Regular people led the call to worship, read the psalm, introduced communion, offered a prayer of invocation, led us in body prayer, and gave the announcements. The contributions of all these different people help us create an atmosphere where participation is the expectation. When the interactive sermon is set in that context, people are ready to take part.

At times there may be no need for a formal sermon. One Sunday night 14 artists from our community put together our worship gathering. They led us in an evening of consideration of the role of the church in history—the good and the troubling—and helped us engage with it through acts of prayer and repentance. The "sermon" was a collection of original art pieces meant to invoke questions, sorrow, joy, and insight. I was asked to lead us in reciting our regular doxology, and I felt the need to put a few additional words around what we were doing that evening. I offered a bit of context for our collective remembering of what had gone on in the life of our faith.

Standing in the doorway so the people lining the hallway and crowding the foyer could hear me, I talked briefly about what it means to seek forgiveness as a community, not just as individuals. These two minutes were an ideal way for me to make a contribution to what we were experiencing without the event having to hinge on a speech. My spoken words were just one element of a much broader expression of faith.

This spirit of contributing—of actively taking part in the life of the church—translates into people who are more inclined to actively participate in the world as God's people. Because they know they have something to offer, they are more likely to offer it freely and regularly in other areas of their lives. When people feel their thoughts are taken seriously in one context, they will carry that confidence into other contexts. Progressional preaching becomes a form of empowerment for people seeking to live in the kingdom of God.

The church isn't meant to be the greenhouse where the life of God is grown in a carefully monitored setting; rather we are to be communities that nurture "kingdom of God horticulturalists" who can recognize the things of God wherever they are growing and foster their growth. Horticulturalists understand plants—what they look like, what will grow in particular environments. Horticulturalists can tell a weed from a plant and are able to give advice on bringing each type of plant to its fullest. Our preaching ought to create communities of people who engage in the world, who recognize the kingdom of God when we find it, and who engage in helping that life grow.

CHAPTER 27

THE NEED FOR NEW SKILLS

Recently, I was in a conversation where I was suggesting that the speaching act is disruptive to the creation of communities of faith. The person I was talking to said, "I agree that people in the churches have a lot more to say than we give them credit for. But when I hear you talk like this, the only thing I can imagine is a bad version of a Brethren meeting."

What this person was getting at is that an open-ended, free-form discussion won't lead to the kinds of communities we are seeking to be any more than speaching does. He's right. Most of our churches don't know how to do progressional dialogue. But just as people have been successfully socialized to sit still and be quiet in church, we can show them how to have constructive, meaningful dialogue.

The skills that need to be developed are those that allow for constructive interaction. The progressional element means we help one another and add to each other's thinking. We shouldn't be satisfied with a bunch of people sharing their opinions and staying right where they were when they started. Progressional preaching is not opinion gathering. It's perspective altering. We invite other opinions to be heard not simply so they'll feel "listened to" but because we all need to hear what is being said. We listen to each other with the understanding that the comments of others force us to be involved in the real world of their experiences. The reason we listen is not only for their benefit, but also for ours.

CHAPTER 28

TOO MUCH INPUT

Between the people contributing to the sermon preparation and the people taking part in the sermon discussion, there are a lot of ideas and opinions involved in progressional dialogue. When people hear me talk about communities teaching and being led by one another, they often ask, "How do you control all that content?" While some ask this question out of a fear of losing control over the message, I find most are asking a legitimate logistical question. They worry that with so many people offering ideas, hopes, and dreams, there won't be the time or the mechanism for everyone to share. They sense that this could quickly turn into an unproductive, devolving group discussion.

In my experience it's rarely a problem that too many people feel frustrated because they never get a word in. No, the bigger problem is that speaching has led a great majority of people in the church to believe that they have nothing to say. So the move to a progressional approach involves helping people develop the competencies and confidence to contribute. Christian formation requires that people not only receive well, but also give well.

CHAPTER 29

DISSENSION

The issue of being a community of people who listen to one another as a Christian practice was recently challenged in a conversation. The person I was talking with had life experiences that led him to concerns that are the opposite concerns of mine.

My friend is 30 years my senior and has a much broader perspective and history than I do; I have much to learn from him. His experience growing up was that his church culture tended to repress personal expression in the name of some sort of groupthink. He has vivid memories of people wanting to say something that God may have intended them to say, but the culture of the church kept anyone from disrupting the status quo. The independent speech was the only way for someone to stand up against the groupthink. For him the strong, independent speaching act is necessary for his faith. As we talked, we agreed to refer to our different perspectives as "allergies." We are both allergic to something. For me it's control of the individual over the group. For him it's control of the group over the individual.

Both of these concerns are dealt with in mandatory, appropriate dissension. Dissension is crucial to progressional preaching. Every suggestion—even those of the pastor—

needs to be properly understood as not eliminating contrary opinions. One of the ways we may want to judge the health of our communities is by our ability to take in—and live with—contrary opinions.

CHAPTER 30

IMPROVISATION

My original mentor in ministry is a man named Brian Doten. In many ways we are different people. The ways we think and react are at times completely opposite; this is one of the reasons he's been such a good mentor.

I remember the time I realized just how different we are. Brian, his wife Chris, my wife Shelley, and I were going to meet another couple and take a walk around one of the lakes in Minneapolis. As we neared the lake, Brian became really quiet and stopped engaging in our conversation. Shelley asked him what he thinking about. His answer was so strange to me. He said, "I'm thinking about what I'm going to say to Bob and his wife when we walk." I thought for a moment and then said, "You mean you're scripting our conversation?" He admitted that was essentially what he was doing, and the three of us spent the next several minutes good-naturedly teasing Brian about it.

A few years later I was in a van traveling across the country with nine other people. We were using one of those 101 questions kinds of books to help pass the time. One of the questions was, "Do you practice phone conversations in your mind before you make a call?" All but three of us did. I was amazed. As a person who is very comfortable with free-form conversation, I'd thought only a small group of people felt the need to plan these kinds of things in advance. I have since realized that I am the one in the minority.

This realization is front and center when I talk about progressional preaching, where it's essential for the conversation to be spontaneous and unplanned. I've tried to think about what this would feel like to someone like Brian or to the other people in that van. The key is for pastors to learn the art of improvisation. Like classically trained musicians who venture into jazz music, pastors don't need to abandon what they know to move into progressional preaching. In fact, the more they know about theology, community, and spiritual formation, the more natural this transition will be.

Tim Lyles is part of our community at Solomon's Porch. He's also a professional musician and music instructor. I asked him to share his insights on improvisation in jazz music. Not surprisingly, there are important parallels for pastors. Here's Tim:

> To the uninitiated listener jazz music often gives the impression that anything goes, chaos is the rule, and performers are playing any random thing that pops into their heads. This misguided impression comes from being exposed to only the simplest, sugar-coated music: music that deals in mostly the two basic tonalities [major and minor], melodies that stay contained within the "do re mi" scale, and rhythms that are so primal that there can be no mistake where the "1...2...3...4" is. Simple is

good, and there is some jazz that covers that base nicely, but jazz music is expansive and moves beyond simple idioms.

Jazz music is most commonly typecast by only one characteristic: improvisation. A lot is made of this aspect, but that emphasis can cause people to overlook the other elements that typify jazz. That's not to say improvisation is not an important element of jazz. Improvisation in jazz means injecting a personal interpretation into an old "standard" tune of the musical canon or even an original piece and using the internal structure of the chord changes over which solos are taken by members of the band.

Of course a musician has to be a very strong technical player before he or she can improvise well. Improvising a solo means stepping out into thin air without having much preknowledge of what is about to be played. There is typically a deep knowledge of the chords and form of a piece [numbers of measures, repeated phrases] nurtured by years of melodic and motific conditioning, but specifically what will unfold in a solo is a mystery to all involved.

Jazz players place great emphasis on being able to read music accurately, being able to navigate complex chord changes, knowing internally a large repertoire of hundreds of standard tunes, and being able to instantly transpose them into any key and interpret them in a variety of styles. Other styles of popular music put great emphasis on the song itself: the melody and lyrics, the meaning of the words and what emotions they invoke. An instrumental solo is merely a diversion in the arrangement. In jazz it's often the other way around. The song is often merely a vehicle for the performer's interpretation. After the melody and form of a song have been stated, the solos are typically the centerpiece, the meat of the expression, before the melody is restated and the arrangement ends.

When not soloing, musicians are judged by their ability to support the solo, to anticipate where it's going, and to complement it. There is a skeletal structure being followed, but there is great liberty for all instrumentalists within that structure. This lends itself to a conversational quality as the performers interact. The soloist can influence the accompanists and vice versa.

For the audience, even those who don't know all that much about music, there is an implicit recognition when a soloist is playing it safe by using a vocabulary of familiar licks and patterns and a visceral thrill when a soloist is exploring unfamiliar territory.

The connection to improvisational preaching is evident. When we take the floor, we "solo," not in an effort to stand alone but to contribute to what has been and is being said. The idea of preaching without "sheet music" is not the same as being untrained or providing thoughts off the cuff.

Instead it's the gift of one who is so well-trained and proficient that she can explore what lies beyond the practiced and planned.

Perhaps the most important part of this improvisational attitude is to know yourself well and have a clear picture of your input. This is where having confidence that the other person has as much to offer you as you do them plays its part. In some ways this is what Brian was doing on our way to meet Bob. It wasn't that he wanted to control the conversation or be the only one talking. He wasn't preparing for a speech; he was trying to be sure he understood himself so he could contribute to the conversation. I guess this is what people do when they prepare for a phone call as well. They aren't planning so they can be the only one talking; they're planning precisely because the other person will be talking as well.

CHAPTER 31

PREPARATION

Because it involves the whole community, there are those who believe progressional preaching is a cop-out, a way of getting other people to do the real work of creating the sermon. But I've found that progressional dialogue requires far more preparation than speaching.

At the same time, it's a very different kind of preparation. It's not the pyramid-building approach—unarguable, one-way assertions presented as well-constructed monuments of thought. Instead it involves knowing the story of God and faith in such a way that the pastor can connect it to the world in which we live. My sermon preparation time requires less crafting of sentences and arguments but far more thought on embodying the story.

I was talking about preaching with Kurt, a friend who pastors a young adult "church within a church" that has nearly one thousand people in worship each week. He said, "You know what is so weird for me when I prepare for a sermon? I read a bunch of perspectives on the topic or passage and then basically pick one or two and present those. I know there are other perspectives on this, and when the people of my church run into these other options, I wonder if they say, 'That is not what I heard at church.'"

Kurt has identified the main problem with having a single spokesperson for the faith. Our faith is too broad and too good to be summed up in only one person's telling. When we allow others to join in the process of creating and guiding our conversation, we're able to preach in a more Christian way. This may mean that we are preaching in a less sectarian way, but it may well be a more Christian way.

I preach without notes, something I have found to be very helpful in setting myself in a position of openness to the community. But this means I have to know my thoughts on the topic much better than if I were using notes. This is one of the reasons our Tuesday night Bible discussion group is so helpful to me. I am able to broaden my understanding of the sermon topic through the input of others and take the rest of the week to really let these ideas stir around in my head. Most weeks the sermon occupies my thoughts in ways that often surprise me. I find I'm much more tuned into the work of God because I'm actively seeking the implications of what I'll be talking about on Sunday night.

Naturally, the no-notes nature of the sermon means it can turn at any point during my monologue. And that comes with its own frustrations. There are times when I had some great thought during the week, but in the midst of my fast talking I forget to mention it. But the times of frustration are relieved by the benefit of the people of our church knowing, partly because of my modeling, that they can give input, even if they don't have a well-crafted statement.

This isn't just helpful for them. I can't tell you how thrilling it is when I am implicated anew during the sermon. Having spent most of my week stewing the sermon in my brain, I am awed by the insights of people who are thinking about these things perhaps for the first time. It is a weekly reminder to me that I have much to learn about the ways of God and the life to which I am being called alongside my community.

This kind of preparation requires the preacher to have an intimate relationship not only with the text, but also with the people. This notion of communal preparation means we must call the people into action not only by asking them to respond to the sermon when it's been presented, but also by asking them to take an active role in the preparation.

I've mentioned the Bible discussion group in several places in this book, but I haven't said much about what it looks like. In part I can't because it looks different from week to week depending on who shows up. Some weeks it's a lively discussion where we have a hard time agreeing on what a passage or story in the Bible has to say to us. Other weeks we are all profoundly moved by the insights of one person and spend our time digging into these ideas. But the details are less important than the fact that this is how we do sermon preparation in our community.

The idea that I can sit alone in front of my computer and see all the complexities of the Bible reeks of arrogance. I need the people of my community to help me find the places that trip them up, the places that confuse them, even the places where they think they understand what's being said but aren't sure what to do about it. In fact, I find it's often when I hear the thoughts of others that I find the places that confuse and trip me up. They help draw me into the story in ways I couldn't navigate on my own. I can't rightly sit in the middle of these people on a Sunday night and presume to know all that God has for them. Their experiences with the Bible and the story of God are as valid as my own.

One night at the Bible discussion group, we were in the midst of our conversation about Mark 5. There were 18 people in the discussion, and at one point I realized I was the only one taking notes. Most weeks when we start the discussion group, I give a bit of context to what we're doing. I say we aren't meeting to study the Bible but to enter into discussion with it and with one another and that the content of our discussion will be carried over to a coming Sunday in a larger conversation during our worship gathering.

It's not all that odd for me to take notes. I try to quote these people during the sermon, but there are so many good things said during our two hours of discussion, there's no way I could remember it all. But what struck me on this particular night was that I was the *only* one taking notes. I didn't want to miss what the people of my community had to say about the content of the coming sermon.

I hadn't anticipated this feeling when we started the church. I didn't know I was going to listen so intently to our people. It's something I've grown into. Maybe I've just been blessed to be part of an amazing community. But they say such insightful and wonderful things, it's become natural to want to capture as much of it as possible.

This part of the preparation process is one of the more unique characteristics of our community, but it isn't a radical idea. I'm just suggesting what is normally done between the pastor and a commentary be done between the pastor and the community. The commentary can be part of that conversation, but it's not the only outside contributor. In reality most pastors aren't nearly as dependent on commentaries as we think we are. When pastors read commentaries, we rarely copy down word for word what they say and then repeat that in the sermon. We think on what we've read, pray about it, and seek to understand how those comments and understandings fit with life as we know it.

It makes sense to use this same process for the comments of the people of our communities. We don't let every comment go by unchallenged or accept everything as an inarguable truth. We take it in, play with it, challenge it with our own structures, then see how it fits the life we are trying to live.

CHAPTER 32

RELATIONSHIP WITH THE BIBLE

The rise of gifted speachers who deliver well-crafted messages of faith and life has had many unfortunate side effects. One I find particularly ironic is the way speaching has promoted a certain kind of relationship with the Bible. Rather than helping people become more tuned in to the Bible, speaching has created a distance between Christians and Scripture. Because they know they'll be told what is important each week, many Christians feel little need to explore the Bible on their own. Because speaching signals a general mistrust in the layperson's ability to understand the things of God, many Christians believe they are incapable of taking much from the Bible.

At the same time, these same Christians tend to believe they know and understand Scripture because they've heard it presented so many times. In reality these people aren't so much biblically literate as they are sermon literate. The speaching act is so well-received in our culture that it carries more weight in people's memory and faith than the story itself. A man in our community put it this way: "When I read the Bible all the way through, I am as surprised by what's *not* in there as by what is."

During one Tuesday night Bible discussion group we were talking about Mark 5 and the story of Jesus casting unclean spirits into a herd of swine. Several of us—maybe even all of us—remembered that the owners of the pigs were upset by the financial loss that resulted when the pigs drowned in the lake. But when we read the story, we found no reference to people being upset by such a thing. Nor is it in the accounts of this story found in Matthew 8 or Luke 8. This came as a bit of a shock to all of us. We had heard sermons that referenced this "fact" and were quite certain this was an important part of the story. A few people were so bothered they could hardly admit it wasn't in the story. We looked in multiple translations and even did an online search to try to find an explanation, but we came up empty.

I see how this could happen. We live in a culture where financial implication matters, so wondering if the owners of the swine would be bothered is the right kind of question for pastors to ask. So they ask it in the sermon. But the thoughts of the speaker and the story itself are so tightly wound together that the hearer has a difficult time separating them.

There are whole generations of people who've been taught a sermonized version of faith from the time they were children. As a result they've developed a taste for sermoniza-tion: Without the pastor's interpretation they have a hard time understanding or entering into the story. This kind of sermonized faith works within the tightly held constructs of speaching, but it has a terribly difficult time in the complex settings of real life. So these people leave church after a really good speach feeling like their faith has been strengthened. But when they try to put those same ideas into play in the real world, they can't quite figure out how to do it. They begin to think *they* are the problem, that if they just had more understanding or a stronger faith, then they would know how to live what they believe. I've heard these people express their frustration, saying things like, "I wish I could remember what the pastor said about that passage," or, "It made sense when the pastor said it, but now I'm not sure I get it." This is not a good sign.

CHAPTER 33

THE BIBLE IN SPEACHING

Unfortunately, the Bible has been caught in a sad, guilt-by-association relationship with speaching. There are those who recognize the introduction of the Bible into a conversation as an indication that a speech is coming and therefore as a signal that any real dialogue is about to come to a halt. I know this because my 13-year-old son, Taylor, is one of them.

One night at dinner Shelley and I were talking with our three sons, Taylor, Ruben, and Chico, about their responsibility to one another. I was trying to make the point that we are called to be "our brother's keepers." I wanted them to see the ramifications of looking out only for themselves or seeing others as competition, so I went to our bookcase and got a Bible. I was intending to read the story of Cain and Abel, but as soon as he saw the Bible, Taylor said, "Oh boy, here comes a speech."

Our children have had very few experiences with true speaching, so I was a little surprised at this reaction. But at age 13, Taylor had already concluded that any conversation involving the Bible was something different. We all laughed a bit when he said it, but it was also troubling to me that my child would see the Bible in this way. Maybe it's the idea that pulling from an outside source—especially one that is understood to be from God—changed the nature of the conversation. But I sure would have hoped for a different response.

Progressional preaching allows us to have a different relationship with the Bible. This approach frees the Bible from being little more than God's declaration of how things are. As preachers we know this. We have engaged with the Bible in ways that others in our churches have not. We know the many styles of literature that make up Scripture. We know some of the Bible is meant to be descriptive while other parts are prescriptive, and we're careful not to confuse the two. But many of the people in our churches don't. So we need to show them. We need to model and live a faith where the Bible has a more authoritative role than that of a cold, dead record of the past.

CHAPTER 34

THE BIBLE AS COMMUNITY MEMBER

The Bible ought to live as an authoritative member of our community, one we listen to on all topics of which she speaks. Understanding the Bible as a community member means giving the Bible the freedom to speak for herself. Sometimes that will mean getting out of the way and putting less effort into interpreting Scripture for others, instead letting them carry out their own relationship with what the Bible says.

Other times we may need to offer some assistance to help others interact with the Bible. But even in these situations, we should think of ourselves as part of a three-way conversation. There are times when I've been sitting with two friends who are talking, and it becomes clear to me that one friend did not understand the other. So I've said, "You know, maybe I could give some context to what she is saying and why she is saying it." It's not as though my friend couldn't speak for herself, but I knew her background in a way that the other friend did not, and I felt I could help clarify the situation. Then there are times when I hear what the friend says, and I feel the need to offer my input, not just to bring clarification but to actually make a suggestion about the implications of what's being said.

This is how I see the role of preaching the Bible. The Bible is really good at speaking for herself, but there are times when the other persons in the dialogue don't know enough about the context and situation to make sense of what they hear. It's during those points when I insert myself into the conversation to offer clarification. Then there are times when the Bible is finished talking, and it becomes my time to share my take on it. I try hard not to confuse the two. In other words, when I'm trying to bring clarification, I'm careful not to insert my take on the passage but rather offer some biblical history or cultural context to help the passage make sense. When I'm sharing my input, I'm careful to do more than clarify what the Bible says and state clearly, "It seems to me this passage has something to say to us."

Most of the time, however, I believe the preacher's role is to let the Bible speak for herself. Too often speaching turns us into the obnoxious boyfriend who never lets his girlfriend say anything. It's not uncommon for people to ask a pastor, "What does the Bible say about such-and-such?" or, "What does God think about such-and-such?" In our desire to provide clear and accessible answers to these questions, we often oversimplify our response or give little more than our take on it, from our theological perspective, and may well have left the Bible out entirely.

In truth the answer to nearly every question of this kind is, "The Bible says a lot of things." In fact, nearly every command, story, instruction, or description in the Bible is part of a larger story intended for a larger purpose. So when we seek to preach the Bible, we are called to preach in a way that opens others to the layers of messages and meaning. Contrary to our fears, people actually appreciate knowing the Bible is complicated and sometimes difficult to understand. These same people try to read the Bible at home and beat themselves up because they can't make sense of what they've read. When we offer simplified explanations for something that scholars and theologians have wrestled with for centuries, we not only strip people of the ability to read the Bible with some semblance of confidence but we also strip the Bible of her richness and beauty.

CHAPTER 35

PROVISIONAL STATEMENTS AND AUTHENTICITY

Progressional preaching involves more than merely tacking a question-and-answer session onto the end of a speached sermon. It takes a whole new attitude on the part of the pastor, one that suggests authentic openness and interest in taking part in an ongoing dialogue with the congregation. It takes a new attitude on the part of the congregation as well, one that suggests authentic transparency and a willingness to live their lives in the open. Both parties need to be sincere about seriously considering what the other person is suggesting, knowing the other could hold a helpful perspective endorsed by God.

I have seen several attempts at "interactive" sermons that fall far short of progressional dialogue, primarily because they were still framed around the idea that there are experts and then there are the rest of us. Often these "special sermons" involve inviting guests to make presentations about topics that are controversial in the church. For example, in recent years some churches have begun inviting people of other faiths to join them for a Sunday in the name of developing a better understanding of these different worldviews. These topical "debates" between Christians and other faiths rarely reach the depth of progressional preaching. They may serve as more interesting forms of speaching, but they are not progressional preaching because there is no expectation that anyone is going to change. Churches who invite atheists or Muslims to come and speak don't believe their people will change faiths as a result of what they hear—few churches would risk this exposure if they believed their own people would convert to other faiths. This "conversation" is really an opportunity to better understand the perspective of these other religions so the church will know how to respond. It's as though we're standing our ground, but we want to know enough about the other guy to make him give up his position.

Real progressional dialogue doesn't necessarily mean a person needs to be converted to the other person's view, but it does need to be an option. If there is no chance of anyone moving a bit, then the dialogue is actually a classic debate, where sides are presented and no one is changed.

The requirement for progressional preaching is that you hold the idea, at least for a bit of time, as a legitimate possibility. The sermon ought to make that happen. The sermon ought to take something that one wouldn't know or think important and put it on people's minds. I see my role in the dialogue as being the one who sets the general parameters for the conversation. So I talk for a while, then I invite others to comment, ask questions, offer clarifications, and so on. If I've done my job, people are thinking and talking about faith issues in a new way, and that thinking will lead them to new considerations.

I've found there to be a few ways to encourage people to talk. The most important is the use of provisional language. This is a skill that will take some time for pastors to learn but one that is undeniably valuable, not just in progressional preaching but also in all of our interactions with others.

When I bring up an idea, I frame it with a phrase like, "It seems to me" or "This is my take on it" or "From the perspective I have." This language is helpful for both the community and for me. It reminds and reinforces the reality that we always speak from our own perspectives. This does not undermine or detract from the importance or authority with which a person speaks. In fact, it strengthens it. When we realize we all hold our convictions, ideas, and desires in a certain context, it gives them meaning.

The use of provisional statements is also important for the other people in the conversation. For some it keeps them from slipping into unnecessary arguments in their heads. This is particularly true for me. I'm a contrarian; when I hear someone say something dogmatic that's just so clearly (from my perspective anyway) *not* the way it is, my natural response is to say, "Well, that's not right." But when others use provisional statements, it helps me remain open to what they're saying, even when I disagree, because their language makes it clear that they're offering an opinion, not trying to force a point on me. Since I'm not the only contrarian in my community, I know it's essential for me to use this language to help others truly consider what's being said and encourage them to respond in kind.

Provisional language is also helpful to those who worry about what others will think about them if they speak. It allows them to frame their ideas as just that—ideas—rather than feeling like they'll have to back up their comments with concrete facts or expert opinions. It gives them permission to have confidence in their thoughts as wonderings inspired by God, wonderings deserving of consideration by the whole community.

I'm not suggesting a person shouldn't have deep beliefs, convictions, assertions, or opinions. Quite the opposite. People should be confident in what they believe but understand their beliefs have come out of a context, a context that is always subject to change. Many of the people in our community, and in most churches, have experienced startling moments of contextual change in their lives. A parent dies, a spouse leaves, a job ends, or an illness strikes, leaving us with little choice but to live in a new context with new assumptions and new beliefs. The posture of provisional statements is a way of honoring the contextual changes life brings with vulnerability and truthfulness.

My son, Taylor asked me if his mom and I would ever get a divorce. This question wasn't hypothetical; it came from a real context because all of Taylor's good friends' parents are divorced. Literally. Of the seven guys he hangs around the most, Taylor is the only one whose parents are still married. So Taylor wanted to know if what was normal for his friends would ever happen to him.

This wasn't the first time he'd asked this question, but I knew this was different. When he was five and asked me the same thing, it was in the context of having just learned of divorce. He wondered if it was something we would do, but there was no pain with it; it was just a curiosity. At 13, however, his question was coming from the realization that many of his friends rarely see their dads, that their weekends are busy and filled with the stress that comes from living in two places and having to coordinate schedules, that some of his friends were having a hard time with their moms dating. This time Taylor's question was asked in the context of pain, of need.

When Taylor was five, I answered the question with a nice, firm, unqualified "No." This is what he needed to hear at the time. In fact, it was all he could hear. He'd heard of divorce, but he didn't have the categories to understand it. It was totally out of his experience. But this time when he asked, his experience was ripe with the reality of divorce. In fact, he may understand it better than I do—he and his friends live it every day. So I knew my answer had to be more honest, more real, more contextual.

In some ways I was surprised by my response. I said something to the effect of, "Taylor, your mom and I have no plans, considerations, or expectations that we will ever divorce. But it could happen. I hope, pray, and work so that it won't. At this point you have nothing to worry about; we are more committed to each other than at any other time in our marriage. But divorce is a reality, and marriage has no guarantees." As I finished, I was worried that such a qualified, potentially ambiguous response would cause doubt in Taylor. Instead I saw in Taylor a sense of confidence. He already knew divorce was a possibility, even if it were a remote possibility. His experience had taught him that divorce is something that can happen to any family. I think deep down he was checking to see if what I would tell him would fit with his understanding of reality. He wanted to know if I would tell him the truth.

The people who sit in our churches expect to hear truth from us as well. They rightly expect us to help them make sense of the realities of their lives—the losses and pains and joys. At the same time, most people recognize that there are no blanket statements to cover the whole spectrum of human experience. The use of provisional statements allows us to offer our thoughts and beliefs in such a way that those involved in the conversation can hold them up to their realities and see how they fit. Rather than rejecting our message, they can see it for what it is—an effort to engage in the profound realities of life and faith.

A woman in our church, Jenell, from our community, who I mentioned earlier, recently blogged about the impact of provisional statements on her faith journey:

> At my church the pastor asks us to practice linguistic humility, saying, "It seems to me" when we speak of God and of the Bible, acknowledging that we speak from our own perspective and do not speak for God. It's helpful to do this in relationships, too, saying, "It seems to me that your biases are affecting your

reading of Scripture here" or "It seems to me that you might want to think about making a different choice next time." We also ask questions: "What would your life be like if you stopped doing this or that?" "Can you imagine pursuing wholeness in this or that way?" I have an codependent addict in my life right now, and a shrink told me to affirm and bless her good choices and help her imagine healthy futures. That would be a good role for me, seeing as I can't control her choices at all. I think we can do that for each other.

—*jenellparis.blogspot.com*

This way of interacting with one another is perhaps the most essential step in moving toward progressional preaching, for it creates an atmosphere of humility and interdependence. It is the way we tell each other, "We are in this together."

CHAPTER 36

TONE OF VOICE

There is more to progressional dialogue than the words we say and who says them. The *way* we say them also matters. There are people who seem to cut off any discussion just by their tone of voice. Maybe you know people who speak in such a way that they move from one topic or sentence to another so quickly or forcefully that it's hard to break in. They may not mean to do it, but they dominate the conversation just by their style.

I struggle with this. I have this fast-paced way of talking, and when I feel like I'm on a roll, I talk even faster. And when my mouth is going fast, my mind gets going faster, and I start talking even more quickly. I'm one of those people whose mind is engaged from the moment I start talking. It's almost a simultaneous act where I'm not always sure what I'm going to say until I'm saying it. So I like the feeling of talking fast; it makes me feel like I'm thinking fast. But the pace of my talk creates little chance for others to contribute.

This doesn't help to create progressional conversation—in interpersonal interaction or in preaching. I've had to work hard to find ways for progressional dialogue to take place. I've had to create systems and practices for taking the conversation beyond where I might otherwise bring it naturally. One could argue that in doing this I'm acting in an unnatural way. But I think that's a good thing. Preaching is a communal act that ought to take us beyond what we might otherwise do naturally.

There was a time when a person in our church told me I have a preaching voice. She said I spoke in a certain tone of voice when I preached. It really bothered me. After fighting off the inclination to be insulted—because I had worked so hard *not* to have a different voice when I preach—I spent a considerable amount of time thinking about this and listening to myself. I have concluded that I do have a "preaching voice," but I use it in other settings as well. For me it comes out when I get excited and energized about something. But I've also noticed that when it comes out in regular conversation, the conversation changes. It becomes, and I become, more intense, more combative, more argumentative.

There is an upside to an excitable speaking style. It tends to draw people in and creates an invitation to join in with the pastor's enthusiasm and passion. But I have to work hard to be sure my excitement doesn't become a deterrent to the very connectedness I'm hoping to create.

CHAPTER 37

PHYSICAL SETUP

A friend said to me, "It sounds like what you're looking for in this kind of preaching is the big-table feel." While I'd never thought about it that way, I think he's right. There's a way people relate to and learn from one another when they're sitting around a table. The way a conversation works around a table is different from a lecture format, so much so that many professional conferences I've attended use this phrase to distinguish between different kinds of seminars. "Main Sessions" tend to mean centralized presentations and "Roundtable Discussion" usually means we all get to share. I'm advocating a way of meeting as communities of faith that use the "Roundtable" sensibilities more often than the "Main Session" style.

The physical setup of a church says a great deal about where the power lies. The pastor—who is elevated on a raised stage, who has a special place set aside for preaching, who has access to the only microphone in the room—clearly holds the power. At our church we meet in the round, and this is very important for us, but I know of other churches that accomplish the "Roundtable" feel in other ways. Some churches use café tables even while maintaining a focus on the stage at the front of the room. In these settings people are encouraged to interact with one another around the table where they are sitting. Other churches put the musicians in the back while the presenter is in the front. This creates the feel of the congregation being in the midst of what happens. I know pastors who walk around the room, up and down the aisles, making eye contact.

These efforts to move the presentation, and therefore the power, are not always easy for people to handle. I preached two consecutive Sundays at a church with a large worship center that seats nearly 2,000 people. The second week I wanted to experiment with something: I wanted to see how the sermon would work if I delivered it from the balcony. The room is quite high-tech and has TV cameras for projecting the image of the preacher onto two large screens on either side of the stage. So the people are not only used to having the preacher in front of them, but also seeing to him in two different sizes.

The sermon was going to focus on Jesus shifting the center of God's activity out of the temple and into the places of the ordinary people, so I felt this change of position would amplify the message of the sermon. But due to limitations with the video equipment and some apprehension from the church staff, we decided to do only the first few minutes of the sermon from the balcony, and then I would move to the front. I loved it. I felt like the message and the method were complementary.

When the time for the sermon came, I positioned myself in the balcony and faced the people sitting there. I can't begin to describe the looks on the people's faces. Many people sit in the balcony because they enjoy the distance from the preacher, and here I was within a few feet of them. I also noticed the people on the main level had a hard time knowing what to do. Should they turn around or not? In both services most of the people on the main level sat facing forward and looked at an empty stage and dark screen. Instead of turning around, they kept to the custom of looking forward. At one point I even said, "I'm up here, behind you—in the balcony," to no avail. I later made my way to the stage, and when I arrived, the congregation applauded. I think the applause was both because they understood the connection of the method and message and also because things were back to normal.

For many of us there is no getting around the fact that we need to utilize lighting and sound reinforcement in our meetings. Most buildings are designed for it, the people expect it, and there is only so much change we have the power to make. But we don't have to be controlled by the physical limitations of our spaces. We can use them to create a greater sense of participation. One way of doing this is to call attention to the physical aspects of the space. I sometimes mention the odd phenomenon of sound amplification when I begin speaking. I note how strange it is for people to see me in one place and hear my voice in another. While few people actively think about this when they listen to an amplified voice, nearly everyone has noticed it at some point. Over time they've become accustomed to it and to the distancing effect it has on communication.

My friend Michael Toy and I were talking about these issues and how difficult it is for so many pastors to make a change because the buildings they meet in were designed for a different purpose. He sent me the following e-mail reflecting on some thoughts he had while watching a documentary about Jacques Derrida. (Derrida, who recently died, was one of the foremost French deconstructionist philosophers of the twentieth century.) Michael wrote:

> There are a couple of beautiful moments [in the documentary], and one of them happened when they tried to do the normal "sit the thinker down in a library and have them pontificate" scene. I'll transcribe it here because I think it has a lot to do with the things that should be said about preaching, and because when Derrida said them, I was bowled over as if Jesus himself had said these things.
>
> > *Interviewer: You're very well-known in the United States for deconstruction. Can you talk a little bit about the origins of that idea?*
> >
> > *Derrida: Before responding to this question, I want to make a preliminary remark on the completely artificial character of this situation. I don't know who's going to be watching this, but I want to underline rather than efface our surrounding technical conditions and not feign a "naturality" which does not exist. I've already in a way started to respond to your question about deconstruction because one of the gestures of deconstruction is not*

to naturalize what isn't natural, to not assume that what is conditioned by history, institutions, or society is natural.

Here Derrida refuses to pretend to have a philosophical conversation in front of books but instead insists on beginning the conversation with a recognition of how unnatural it is to be sitting in front of a camera, talking to people who aren't there, and pretending not to be talking to the whole crew who is there.

Similarly, a discussion of preaching needs to begin with what is not natural about the act of preaching, in the setting, in the communications style, and in the relationship between the preacher and the congregation. It also needs to recognize and acknowledge the communal and societal context in which preaching happens, the idolatry of the expert, the passivity of a television-trained congregation, etc.

Anyway, that's my pseudo-intellectual (I can't read Derrida, but I can watch a DVD about him—is that better or worse than Cliffs Notes®?) posturing on preaching for today.

—Michael

This is a call to be prophetic in the deconstruction of the systems of power. When we are willing to notice, point out, and name the issues of power in our settings, we're creating a better situation in which the gospel can be preached.

CHAPTER 38

MICROPHONES AND POWER

There is one element of the physical setup of a church space that nearly every church takes for granted. That's the microphone. Yet this one seemingly innocuous piece of equipment and its ability to allow a single voice to dominate space and time has changed the church and solidified the pervasiveness of speaching.

Microphones, by their very design, take one voice and elevate it above the others. It's meant to help sound go places that it can't go on its own. The microphone differs from an amphitheater or other acoustically sensitive spaces in that most microphones are designed to allow only certain voices to be amplified. There is a decision made as to which voice is amplified and which are not. This creates a structure of power that changes the relationship between those who can be heard and those who cannot. When a voice is amplified to decibels above what is normally possible, we have moved into superhuman communication. I'm not suggesting superhuman communication is always inappropriate; rather we ought to recognize when we are using methods and technologies that change the human and social presuppositions of communication. I don't believe our communities of faith are well-served by utilizing technologies that create this power imbalance if we let them go unchecked or unnoticed.

The use of an amplified voice creates the situation where the recipients are powerless to speak back. What makes this situation even more insidious is when the person with the power of the microphone is also the person who is presuming to speak for God. Not only does this person have the social and spiritual power of being the pastor, who is thought of as being different from the rest of the people, but this person also has the technical power to force others to listen. It could be that what we recognize as effective, powerful speaching is really the result of one person with a microphone dominating a group of people.

In truth this is one of the easiest problems for churches to solve. Most of us, myself included, preach in spaces where some kind of amplification is necessary. It's fairly simple to provide microphones for others to use, either on stands around the room or with area microphones mounted on the ceiling. We can further reduce the sense that all the power belongs to the pastor by turning up the lights when it's time for the congregation to contribute. We can have people who lead prayers or give worship instructions do it from the midst of the people and not from platforms of power.

There are some who have concerns about people speaking and others having a hard time hearing them. While we certainly wouldn't want to make the entire gathering hard to hear, it's possible we put too much emphasis on being sure that hearing comes easily for everyone. When it takes work to hear what is being said, it causes people to listen differently, and that's a good thing. The posture of people sitting up, leaning forward, and straining to hear one another may create in us an outcome we are desperately missing.

CHAPTER 39

LISTENING AS THE PRIMARY SKILL

Speaching has caused speech making to be elevated to one of an "effective" pastor's primary skills. But for all the work involved in developing the skills required to be a good speaker, the most important one is often the most neglected. For speaking—particularly for pastors—involves knowing how to listen. And listening is not simply hearing. It's a practice requiring interpretation, intuition, and openness.

In some ways hearing is the easy part. Our auditory sense is different from the other senses in that it's possible to shut your eyes or plug your nose; you can shut your mouth and keep your hands to yourself. But the ear needs help to stop working. It's as if we are designed to hear without effort; it's trying to *stop* ourselves from hearing that involves work.

But listening—now that's something different. Listening means engaging the whole self. We all learn to function by choosing what to ignore and what to notice in environments where there are multiple stimuli being received by our ears. (In fact there is some interesting work being done on what happens to the stimuli we don't engage with in our active listening. This is the kind of stuff that, 100 years from now, may redefine our understanding of how we gain knowledge.) Listening is an act of attention.

It's also one of the ways we learn. We've all had the experience of sitting in a classroom (or a church or the kitchen) and listening to another person talk about something we find boring. We hear the words coming out of the person's mouth, but unless we really listen and engage our minds with what we're hearing, it doesn't stick. But when we truly attend to something, we remember it and integrate it into our understanding of the world.

Listening is also a way of seeing. When we listen to other people's stories and perspectives, we're brought into their worlds in ways they could never show us. I can't always see someone's pain or joy, but I can usually hear it when I'm listening. Perhaps this is what the apostle Paul was getting at in Romans 10:14-15: "How, then, can they call on the one they have not believed in? And how can they believe in the one of whom they have not heard? And how can they hear without someone preaching to them? And how can anyone preach unless they are sent? As it is written: 'How beautiful are the feet of those who bring good news!'" Would this also mean that we, the preachers, are able to believe when we hear our people preach? Certainly Paul's words are as important for us as they are for "them."

For the bulk of the Bible's existence it has been an oral piece. The notion of reading about faith is the product of our educated twentieth- and twenty-first-century understanding of how we take in information. We need to recognize its unusual place in the history and practice of faith. For every generation of Christians before the modern era the Bible was something they listened to, making them more adept at listening to each other. Now that we read the Bible, we tend to think of it as being in a different class from the Word of God still living in our brothers and sisters. There is a strong tendency to take what we see in the Bible and allow it to trump the validity of what we hear in history and in one another.

There is a strange reference in the book of Revelation that may be instructive on this note:

> Then I heard a loud voice in heaven say: "Now have come the salvation and the power and the kingdom of our God, and the authority of his Messiah. For the accuser of our brothers and sisters, who accuses them before our God day and night, has been hurled down. They triumphed over him by the blood of the Lamb and by the word of their testimony; they did not love their lives so much as to shrink from death."

—Revelation 12:10-11

The blood of the Lamb and the testimony of the saints have been a demonstration of the power of the kingdom of God throughout the history of the church. Should we not find a more integrated and honored place for the testimony of our people? This testimony can certainly move beyond the simple conversion stories that have become trite and over-used in some traditions. This testimony can and should be offered in narratives as complex as the Bible itself. It can and should be listened to with the same sense of respect and reverence as the Bible itself.

Developing the skill of listening is a challenge for the entire community—pastors and laypeople alike. There are those who say they don't naturally possess the ability to listen, interpret, and retell, and they wonder if this progressional preaching approach is for them. Admittedly, it takes some practice and patience to fully integrate this approach into the life of a church. It also takes support. Progressional preaching will need the same investment of resources and training that speaching has received. Many people are not natural speachers. That's why we have seminars, classes, tapes—an entire industry to help nonspeachers become speachers. We've developed the competencies to create in our leaders what isn't there naturally. Let's take this same ability and help one another become progressional communities.

CHAPTER 40

THE VOICE OF THE CHURCH

Perhaps the most basic step in becoming a community that listens well is figuring out where to put our attention. In speaching churches people have been trained to pay attention to the voice of the speacher. Communities moving toward progressional dialogue need to learn how to pay attention to the voices of those who don't usually share.

But it's not enough just to pay attention to others. We have to be willing to be affected by what they say. There will be times when someone's voice moves us from one position to another, but there will also be times when the input of another person helps us solidify our thinking on an issue. In other words, being affected by others doesn't mean we are easily swayed; rather we understand that our perspectives are constantly in need of fine-tuning.

This openness calls us to recognize the presence of God in all people. It's tragic when a person comes to church with a hunch or a sense that God has been leading his thinking on a topic. Yet when he gets to church, he experiences a one-way, well-supported presentation with no chance to respond. It can cause him to believe his intuition or hunch isn't nearly as important as the well-supported sermon.

The irony is that we preachers are often led by just this kind of intuition or hunch. The difference is that we have the time to put our thoughts together and the platform from which to present them. But the layperson with the idea quickly runs out of reasons to bring her ideas with her. She may even stop paying attention to those promptings. Instead she comes as an "empty vessel" and prays she will be able to hear something from God. Over time this act will create in her the belief that what she has to share must take a backseat to what the pastor presents. She is to be the recipient and the speacher is the provider. Even if the words from the mouth of the speacher or on the bulletin insert promise an interactive engagement with God, the fact that her previous engagement with God has had no bearing on what happens to her at church will remind her of her "true" place. If we want people to take part in the full life of the Christian community, we have to give them a voice and then pay close attention to what they say.

Listening to the ordinary. There is a different kind of formation that happens when people believe their ordinary lives are part of what matters not only to God, but also to others. Part of the effect of speaching is that the ordinary in people's lives is often ignored. In progressional preaching the ordinary becomes important in the preaching. It is into, through, and for the ordinary that preaching takes place. The gospel message becomes the intermingling of the ordinary and extraordinary.

The book of Mark tells of Jesus' temptation in the desert. The imagery is rich with Jesus being sent into the desert just as the nation of Israel was sent into the desert. The people of the first century would have understood this not as an unusual experience but an ordinary one of a life lived in the area surrounding them. Then Mark throws in this beautiful image: "[Jesus] was with the wild animals, and angels attended him" (Mark 1:13). This is a wonderful picture of the ordinary and the angelic together. This ought to be the outcome of our progressional preaching—the joining of the ordinary and the special, the life of the people and the life of God.

The practice of listening to the ordinary begins with believing the person has something to share on the topic. This can be a hard shift for some people. The idea that we need to be careful about whom we listen to is deeply embedded in many of us. But to listen to someone doesn't mean we are in agreement on all things. Listening is an active practice that allows us to listen without necessarily being enticed into a completely new position. I know there are ideas and perspectives that aren't useful to a life with God, and it can be compelling to just ignore that which is not preapproved. But in my experience we give up much more when we only stick with what we're sure of than when we open ourselves up to something more.

Listening to the outsider. I have a friend who is quite bothered by a statistic stating that more than 80 percent of people between the ages of 20 and 40 receive their spiritual input from sources outside the church. Certainly he is troubled by the idea that the church isn't doing its job of being engaged with outsiders. But even more bothersome to him is the quality of the information they're receiving.

I also have concerns about the church adequately engaging with outsiders, but I don't share his worry that people are worse off when they receive spiritual guidance outside the church. What a horrible state the church would be in if all her people only saw the life of the kingdom through the eyes of the church. No church, not even all churches combined, have all the truth in the world. If we only looked to the church for answers on how to relate to one another or how to be physically healthy or how to raise our children, we would be missing out on much of what God would have us learn.

One night after church a number of us were eating at our usual spot when we started talking about this book. As we talked about my thoughts on why so many pastors find it difficult to allow for the input of others in their sermons, one guy, Jake, said, "Well, I can see why some would be concerned with what other people might say. You never know, people might have some really strange views." To which Tim, who is probably 20 years older than Jake, said, "And I want to hear every one of them." Tim's life had been full of really good church experiences. He is the father of a young adult daughter and a teenage daughter. And he knows his life is made richer by interacting with as large a cross-section of people as possible. In that moment he served as a mentor to Jake. For Jake to hear this reassurance from Tim—that it's good to hear from others—was more valuable than any words I could write on the topic.

Listening to the unbeliever. No one is considered more "outside" than those who don't share our faith. There are many Christians who might be open to progressional dialogue but fear the input of those outside the church. For them if a person isn't part of the Christian faith, then we shouldn't listen to him on things of faith and the Christian life. In their minds only those who sign on to Christianity have anything important to say about it.

For those who are pursuing a holistic understanding of faith and life, the divide between that which is important to the Christian life and that which is secular isn't significant. When we realize there is no area of our lives that isn't impacted by and impacting our faith, the categories of who can speak into our faith fall away. We listen to unbelievers on everything from the way we spend our money and how we educate our children to the way we care for our bodies and how we interact with the environment. So when the church maintains practices that silence the unbeliever, we reinforce the idea that preaching is intended for the safety of the church, not to help us connect with the full spectrum of our lives.

The question facing churches who choose to listen is, *How willing are we to believe the unbeliever?* This issue will cause us to depend more fully on the work of the Holy Spirit to serve as the One who reminds us of and teaches truth. In John 14 Jesus tells his disciples they must obey all that he taught them, a daunting task in itself. Jesus goes on to say this:

> All this I have spoken while still with you. But the Advocate, the Holy Spirit, whom the Father will send in my name, will teach you all things and will remind you of everything I have said to you. Peace I leave with you; my peace I give you. I do not give to you as the world gives. Do not let your hearts be troubled and do not be afraid. (John 14:25-27)

It's the Holy Spirit who is the arbiter of truth. The peace we have ought to come from the Spirit of God and not from our ability to control who speaks.

One of the frequent statements of Jesus in the Gospels is, "The kingdom of God is like...." Jesus goes on to use the most normal and, at times, mundane parts of culture to explain the kingdom of God. Is it possible that Jesus uses these descriptions not simply as metaphors but because the kingdom of God really is like these things? If so, then we would benefit from listening to those who know about such things. When other contributors to the Bible say we can know about life with God by looking at soldiers, farmers, and athletes (2 Timothy 2:1-7), even ants (Proverbs 6:6-8), we would do well to listen to those who know about these things.

I've found that the fear inherent in opening ourselves up to the voices of others is nearly always unfounded. In fact, time and time again I've seen our community's capacity for understanding and insight. In preparing for our collective discussion one night, I decided to change things from our usual pattern of hearing the story read, giving my contribution to the conversation through a monologue, then opening the floor to responses from others. Instead we heard the reading—a full chapter from one of the gospels—then invited people to share their responses to what had been read. On this particular night I'd put my thoughts and those from the Bible discussion group into a PowerPoint presentation. I planned to use it after the conversational part of the sermon. As people started sharing, I felt this incredible sense of the divine: Nearly everything they said was already on the list of ideas I'd written out. When I finally put the slide on the screens, it was as if I'd performed some mind-reading trick where I'd predicted what people were going to say. It was a formative night for me, one that gave me tremendous confidence in our community. I saw clearly that we have within us all I can come up with and then some.

Listening to the voices of others is an essential part of being the church. We were never meant to close in on ourselves. We were never meant to engage with only those who share our positions. We've been called to live in the way of Jesus, who sought out the ordinary, the outsider, and the unbeliever, not only to make them whole, but also to bring his followers into the fullness of life in the kingdom. For it is often in the life of others where we find God at work in the most profound ways imaginable.

A FEW FINAL THOUGHTS

Thank you for taking time to consider my thoughts on preaching. I hope you've found my contribution to be of value in your life and that you've had as much to say while reading the book as I had in writing it.

You may feel the book came to a rather sudden end, and just like in a conversation you may have wanted to keep going. If that's the case, then I'm glad the book did its job of getting you going. I tried to say at the beginning that this would not be a how-to book but a hard look at the role of preaching in our lives. These deep considerations create conversations that will never truly end.

I'm quite certain you didn't agree with every suggestion I made, and that, too, is a good thing, for I'm not sure I will always agree with what I've written. That is the nature of being people who grow, learn, and become.

I hope the ideas in this book help all of us find ways to live well with our communities and move our preaching to depths of personal engagement that speaching can never reach. Moreover, I hope there will be those among us who will work on the skills of progressional dialogue in preaching in such a way that our children's children will look back upon our time as a period when their ancestors took seriously the call to preach and willingly did the hard work that led to their vibrant faith.

May your life as a preacher be one surrounded by the preachers among us, and may "the message of Christ dwell among you richly as you teach and admonish one another with all wisdom through psalms, hymns and songs from the Spirit, singing to God with gratitude in your hearts" (Colossians 3:16).

WORKS CITED

Kilde, Jeanne Halgren. *When Church Became Theatre: The Transformation of Evangelical Architecture and Worship in Nineteenth-Century America*. Oxford: Oxford University Press, 2002.

Lloyd-Jones, D. Martyn. *Preaching & Preachers*. Grand Rapids, Mich.: Zondervan, 1972.

Miller, Calvin. *Sermon Maker: Tales of a Transformed Preacher*. Grand Rapids, Mich.: Zondervan, 2003.

Rathbun, Russell. *Post-Rapture Radio: Lost Writings from the Failed Revolution at the End of the Last Century*. San Francisco: Jossey-Bass, 2005.

THE FOLLOWING IS AN EXERPT FROM...

Available at your local Christian bookstore or at **www.youthspecialties.com**.

A NEW APPROACH FOR A NEW AGE

Welcome to Solomon's Porch. It is truly an honor to invite you into a week in the life of our community. We hope you will be our guest and find friends and kindred spirits with whom you can journey in the pursuit of life in harmony with God.

Let me make a few clarifications from the beginning. The intention of this book is not to tell you how you can have an effective church in the 21st century. I'm not laying out a how-to guide for reaching "target audiences." I won't even try to convince you that you'd be better off having a church with the practices, intentions, and values of Solomon's Porch. My desire in writing this book is to provide a descriptive glimpse at the efforts of our emerging community on the chance that you will find our story useful as you seek dreams of your own.

This book is more about our community's honest longings and efforts than our accomplishments and results. It is a collection of the hopes and aspirations of a people trying. Our efforts to arrange our lives around communal spiritual formation are, at times, awkward and pathetic. Yet at other times, they are wonderfully forward-leaning and pull us toward God in ways we never anticipated. They are nearly always sincere attempts toward sustainable Christian spiritual formation, utilizing practices that extend beyond the education model of Christian discipleship.

Maybe, like me, you're wondering why I'd write a book when so much of this is in the experimental stage. I've spent many hours struggling with the idea of "selling" what I think of as a vision for Christian community that is God's to give, not mine. What's pulled me through is my belief that there are wonderful people—pastors, teachers, lay leaders, new Christians, lifelong Christians—who are not interested in a model program or approach to spirituality, but are searching the stories of others to find permission to pursue their own deeply held, unspoken intuitions about how faith and church could be. In some ways this book is an act of poetry; it is an attempt to put words around our experiences and desires to allow others to step inside.

In an ideal world this would be a two-way conversation. We would be mutually inspired by sharing our stories, visiting each other's faith communities, eating in each other's homes, and discovering the details of each other's lives. In reality, of course, we have few options beyond visiting Web sites, reading books, and meeting one another at the occasional "New Church Trends" conference. But I hope that this book will inspire you to seek face-to-face conversations with other searchers as you seek ways to make your own dreams of faith become reality.

A NEW APPROACH FOR A NEW AGE

This book will bring you into our community and our life. You will meet our people through journal entries, hear stories from each day of the week, and be invited behind the scenes to see how we are trying to live. First, though, let me explain what lies behind much of the design and practices of our community. In some ways this book is not about the 21st century—it is about the 1880s and the changes brought by the Industrial Revolution.

Beginning with the Industrial Revolution, innovations in travel, communication, and science have changed the way we define community and live in it. Incredible advances in medicine have made life possible where once there was only death. These shifts have changed the way we think about what it means to share our lives with others and how we measure the value of life. We have revolutionized how we live and nearly all that we believe, know, and understand—but much of the thinking and practices of Christianity have stubbornly stayed the same.

It seems to me that our post-industrial times require us to ask new questions—questions that people 100 years ago would have never thought of asking. Could it be that our answers will move us to re-imagine the way of Christianity in our world? Perhaps we as Christians today are not only to consider what it means to be a 21st century church, but also—and perhaps more importantly—what it means to have a 21st century faith. The answers to all these questions will have an impact on how our faith communities are structured, what we do in those communities, and the practices we utilize for spiritual formation. They influence how we experience community in daily life, how we relate to others, our faith and beyond, and even how we understand the gospel itself.

Perhaps most importantly for our conversation in this book, these changes call us to rethink the value of the education model in spiritual formation. The heartbeat of our efforts within Solomon's Porch is to pursue a way of life in harmony with God created from means extending far beyond what educational formation can provide. I do not intend to spend time discussing the failings of the education model, but rather to lean into the future with descriptions of our practices—some tried and true, and some experimental.

Holistic Formation. One notion we are seeking to re-imagine is the whole concept of spiritual formation—how people become Christian and live in faith. In the 19th century it was believed that the most effective way to deepen a person's spiritual life was to increase her knowledge about God. People behaved—and still behave—as though the spiritual part of a person is a separate component that can be worked on and developed in isolation from the rest of the person. This approach has been refined with great fervor over the last 100 years and in some ways has just recently hit its stride.

Our efforts are built upon the assumption that we are able to imagine and create something of greater beauty and usefulness if we move away from speaking of spiritual life in dualistic tones, as if the spiritual part of a person is a separate component that can be worked on and developed in isolation from the rest of the person. We are working with a view of spiritual formation in which we forget about working on a part of a person's life and instead work with people as if there is no distinction between the spiritual, emotional, physical, social, professional, and private aspects of life. We hope the result of this vision of human formation will be a move toward a place where we focus on the holistic formation of people who are in harmony with God in all arenas of life, and who seek to live in the way of Jesus in every relationship, every situation, every moment.

But then again, maybe things are just fine. There could certainly be an argument made that Christianity is doing fine and that we are not in need of this radical re-imagining. It is possible that the way forward centers on the church improving its current approach of education-based spiritual formation. Perhaps all we need is better curriculum and better training for our pastors and teachers. Perhaps we need to make a clearer call for the basics of the faith and be sure that people are well-grounded in their beliefs. Perhaps the church is actually positioned quite well in the post-industrial world, and with some fresh models of teaching and learning, will do just fine.

Perhaps, but I think not, or at least not for us. We join with the many people, professional and lay, who have suggested in writings, conversations, prayers, and pleadings that the Christian Church has not lived up to its potential or calling in the post-industrialized world, but that it could. Maybe there is something to the critique that the church is marginalized in the world to such a degree that the marks of a "successful" church have been reduced to tangible evidence such as size, market share, political influence, healthy budgets, and the creation of model citizens living the American Dream. This marginalization is not due to the Church's poor use of marketing techniques or lack of effort in discipleship. Rather, I've become convinced that our misguided belief that life change can come through proper knowledge acquired through education has failed to produce the kind of radical commitment to life in harmony with God in the way of Jesus that we are called to. When the realities of life crash into our knowledge of God, faith is often the prime casualty. Doesn't the role of communities of faith need to include more than making converts and educating people in right belief? Doesn't it need to also make possible corporate and personal lives lived in harmony with God? I am not suggesting that churches have not sought this holistic approach to faith in other times, but I do believe that the knowledge-based spiritual formation of the 20th century has so reduced the call of Jesus to right belief that many become confused about why mere profession of belief does not bring about life change.

A Holistic approach to community spiritual formation. In some ways it's a bit odd for a church still in its toddler years to discuss its efforts in spiritual formation. This is particularly true for Solomon's Porch because we are very much in the midst of experimenting with the ideas of this book. My intention here is not to create a plan for others to follow, but to invite people into a needed conversation that will continue for decades. To be honest, the legitimacy of what we're doing at Solomon's Porch will be best judged in 15 to 20 years. In some ways it's easy for people who have chosen our community to live out these desires in the short run at this particular stage in their lives. The question that haunts me is not, "Do people like our church?" but "Is there any real formation happening?" Two decades from now, will our efforts at human formation show a contribution to the lives we have led for the past 20 years? Will they have helped us live as blessings to the world, or will we simply be living the kind of self-absorbed "personal" Christian lives that are so common today?

This is the kind of issue that those who buy in to the educational model of spiritual formation may not need to struggle with. The educational approach provides assurances of effectiveness through tests, catechisms, and statements of faith, which measure whether people have been "properly" formed. When we move beyond belief-based faith to life-lived, holistic faith, the only true test is lives lived over time.

Spiritual formation through community. There is a call embedded in Christianity that moves us to life together. This idea of holistic spiritual formation is nothing new. In fact, it has a long and prominent history within the Christian church. Throughout history, becoming a follower of Jesus has often meant being brought into a community of people who eat together, live together, share their possessions and their lives. We will introduce you to our efforts at being a community of people who not only meet on Sundays, but who become deeply connected to one another. I truly believe that community is where real spiritual formation happens. Most people come to faith not by an isolated effort but through living day by day with people of faith such as their families or friends. People may not fully understand the beliefs involved, but they learn what the Christian life looks like as they see people to whom they are deeply connected living out the disciplines of prayer, worship, and service. Nearly every Christian I know grew into the faith long before they knew a whole lot about it. Even for those who first heard the things of Christianity through an isolated presentation of some sort, this was only the start of a life, not the summation of the life. They were just beginning to understand what this was all about. Isn't this what so many of us still experience—a living of our faith before and beyond our understanding of it?

In many ways, becoming Christian is much like learning our native language; we pick it up when we are immersed in it. I would guess that nearly all of us spoke and communicated long before we started our formal education. What we then learned in school was not the beginning of language use, but the refining of it. In educational settings, the theory of language acquisition through immersion is by far the most successful means of learning. So it is with Christian faith. Rather than seeing Christianity as belief we acquire in a completed form, we ought to enter into it with the understanding that we are at the beginning of a life-long process of discovery and change. Ours is a faith that is lived, from beginning to end.

Community as a means of spiritual formation serves to immerse people in the Christian way of living so that they learn how to be Christian in a life-long process of discovery and change. Christian community can and should be context for evangelism and discipleship, a place where faith is professed and lived.

The word community has become the buzzword of the day. Part of the problem with buzzwords is that their overuse can leave them with virtually no meaning at all. In our current vocabulary, community can mean everything and nothing at the same time. It can mean people who live on the same street, or people of a similar ethnic background, or people who think the same way about issues. As we of Solomon's Porch understand the term, Christian community has four functional elements: Local, Global, Historical, and Futurical.

By local community, we mean the people with whom we live in physical proximity. It includes the people we live near, work with, drive past, and stand next to in line. It includes those we choose to recognize and those we do not. I find it's often the case that people use the word community to refer to those who are most like them. But the story of God from Abraham to Jesus calls us to a deeper understanding of "our neighbor" that embraces those who are not like us at all—and those with whom we worship week by week.

Oddly, many Christians find that their fellow congregants play no more crucial a role in their daily lives than the people they walk past in the grocery store. They share a common experience from time to time and receive services from the same organization, but little else. The people of Solomon's Porch seek to make community mean something in our Christian context, so we look for ways to make our community of faith a place where we become involved in one another's lives in intimate, meaningful, transformative ways.

This kind of intimacy requires us to move beyond mere accountability. Accountability is built on the notion that a person will do her own work as she seeks to live a Christian life while others do what they can to keep her on track. This may seem like the best our local community can offer us, but we are striving for more. We feel called to vulnerability. We are seeking to move into relationships where we don't merely ask others to hold us to living in the way of Jesus, but where we invite them to participate in our efforts to do so. We are trying to open our lives up in such a way that others do not simply keep us on track, but become actual agents of redemption and change.

We also understand ourselves as part of a global community. We are required to live our local expressions of Christianity in harmony with those around the world. The beliefs and practices of our Western church must never override or negate the equally valid and righteous expressions of faith lived by Christians around the world. It's essential that we recognize our own cultural version of Christianity and make ourselves open to the work of God's hand in the global community of faith.

Christian community also includes those who have come and gone before us—our historical community. Just as with local and global communities, there are elements of our historical community that we may well find difficult to stomach, such as the excesses of the Crusades or the Salem witch trials. Though we are not called to live the faith of the past, and we need to be people of faith of our day, our current and future vision for the church cannot be formed without a sense of the visions of the past. It is through our historical community that we are reminded, guided, taught, and led in the ways of God. We are compelled to enter into the context of those who have served, loved, and believed before us. Therefore we must always ground ourselves in the history and traditions of the Christian community that have come before us. There is one body of Christ through all time, and we are part of that body in our particular place and time. If we separate ourselves from the work of our body in previous times, we do so to our limitation and peril.

It's tempting to let our understanding of community end there, but I believe we are called to live in community with those who come after us as well—with our futurical community. We owe this concept to a 20-year-old named Luke. During a discussion of part of the Bible that I no longer recall, Luke called us all to a life that is future-focused as well as focused on the here and now. He said we are called to live in awareness of the legacy we leave for those who come after us. He said, "What would you call it? Futurical?" And we have ever since.

As we work to create a new way of living in our time, we must also look ahead. Even as we are seeking to create expressions of faith that are meaningful for us in this time and place, we are striving to grow into people who will bless future generations and guide them to do the same for their time and place.

There is something compelling, powerful, and liberating about living life in harmony with God, not in the isolation of an individual relationship ,but as part of a community that includes those around us, those far from us, those who came before us, and those who will come after us. At the center of this holistic, communal approach to spiritual formation is the creation of Christian communities that are a continuation of the story of God, from Abraham to Jesus to today.

The kingdom of God and teaching about Jesus. It seems to me that this call to communal spiritual formation challenges us to re-imagine the gospel itself. Perhaps the challenges of living the dreams of God in the post-industrial world go beyond methodology problems. Perhaps we have been propagating a limited message, reducing biblical authors to sound bytes that cut the gospel message into so many pieces that we are left with little more than statements of what we believe rather than the broader story of how we are to enter into God's story through a life lived in faith.

I readily admit that any attempt to simplify the work of the church over the centuries or the intentions of the apostles of the early church is risky at best. People moving down the road of "summing things up" run the risk of over-simplification and displaying their ignorance in plain view. With this risk squarely in mind, I contend that Kingdom living and following in the way of Jesus are essential to the way we understand the lessons of the New Testament church. There are many of us who have come to believe that the "gospel" that sits at the center of much of Protestant life today is a bifurcated version of the gospel message, one that reduces the call to Kingdom life to simple belief about Jesus while leaving the exemplary Christian life to the very devoted.

Once again, I am not the first person to suggest this. In fact, if you'll allow me to use the following "sound byte" from the end of the New Testament book of Acts, you'll see that these ideas have been present from the beginning of the articulation of the Christian life. The author of the New Testament book of Acts finishes the book by describing the actions of the apostle Paul during his time in Rome at the end of the first century.

> For two whole years Paul stayed there in his own rented house and welcomed all who came to see him. Boldly and without hindrance he preached the Kingdom of God and taught about the Lord Jesus Christ. (Acts 28:30-31)

These words offer a needed understanding of the balance between learning about Jesus and living like him.

There is little question in my mind that many of us in the Protestant church have erred in our overemphasis on teaching about Jesus to the exclusion of the call to the Kingdom life. While this is in no way true in every situation, there are far too many times that we allow ourselves to believe that efforts of education about Jesus are the full extent of evangelism and discipleship. This can be seen in the extraordinary efforts around content creation and delivery in churches today.

The two-handed message of Kingdom life and teaching about Jesus is found throughout the New Testament (and in different forms in the Old Testament) so frequently that I believe the early church saw these as two inseparably linked pillars of the church they intended to build. In many ways it is hard for me to understand how Christianity became so limited and such a far cry from the Kingdom of God life lived in the way of Jesus.

Perhaps another sound byte would be helpful, this time from the life of Jesus. At the beginning of the Gospel of Mark, the author quotes Jesus at the start of his public ministry:

> "The time has come," he said. "The Kingdom of God is near. Repent and believe the Good News!" (Mark 1:15)

When I recently noticed this passage, it became destabilizing for me. I had always understood the "Good News" as summed up in the life, death, burial, resurrection, ascension, and promised return of Jesus. After reading this almost innocuously short passage, however, I started wondering. What was the Good News Jesus was referring to all those years before his death, burial, and resurrection? Could it be that the Good News Jesus talked about was less a call to believe in the things that happened to him or would happen to and through him than an invitation into Kingdom life?

At the same time, it is inspiring and even life-giving to imagine an approach to spiritual formation that can impact us in a pervasive, deeply life-altering way. At Solomon's Porch we are seeking a spiritual formation that, in its essence, is not about individual effort but communal action involving a spirituality of physicality, centered on the way we lead our lives, allowing us to be Christian in and with our bodies and not in our minds and hearts only; a spirituality of dialog within communities where the goal is not acquiring knowledge, but spurring one another on to new ways of imagining and learning; a spirituality of hospitality that is not limited to food before or after meetings, but is intended to create an environment of love and connectedness where people are formed and shaped as they serve and are served by one another; a spirituality of the knowledge of God where the Bible is not reduced to a book from which we extract truth, but the Bible is a full, living, and active member of our community that is listened to on all topics of which it speaks; a spirituality of creativity where creative gifts are not used as content support but rather as an invitation for those so inclined to participate in the generative processes of God; a spirituality of service, which is the natural response of all seeking to live in the way of Jesus and is not reserved for the elite of the faith.

Our hope is that this will be evident in a community not limited to supplemental small-group programs but valued as the cultivating force in which lives with God are the claim and invitation to Kingdom life.

So bring your dreams, passions, and questions, and join us for a week in the life.

At the end of each chapter I would like to share with you a song from our community. This text-only format of music certainly leaves much lacking, but I hope the lyrics will help you catch a bit more of a week in the life of our community.

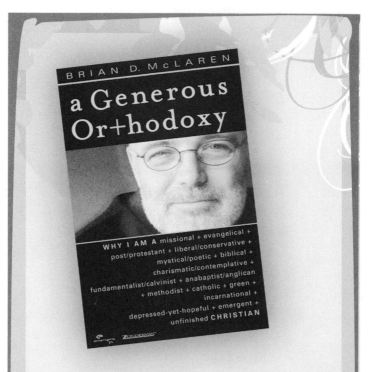

BRIAN D. McLAREN

a Generous
Or+hodoxy

WHY I AM A missional + evangelical +
post/protestant + liberal/conservative +
mystical/poetic + biblical +
charismatic/contemplative +
fundamentalist/calvinist + anabaptist/anglican
+ methodist + catholic + green +
incarnational +
depressed-yet-hopeful + emergent +
unfinished CHRISTIAN

In a sweeping exploration of belief, author Brian McLaren takes us across the landscape of faith, envisioning an orthodoxy that aims for Jesus, is driven by love, and is defined by mission. *A Generous Orthodoxy* rediscovers the mysterious and compelling way that Jesus can be embraced across the entire Christian horizon.

A Generous Orthodoxy
RETAIL $19.99
ISBN 0310257476

Visit **www.emergentys.com** or your local Christian bookstore.

In a conversational
narrative style, author
Dan Kimball guides
church leaders on how
to create alternative
services from start to
finish. He explains why
youth pastors are
usually the ideal staff
to start a new service.

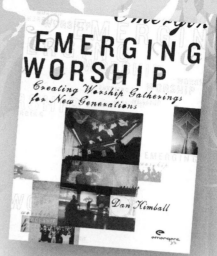

Emerging Worship
Creating Worship Gatherings
for New Generations
Dan Kimball

RETAIL $14.99
ISBN 0310256445

Today's postmodern generation
does not respond to church like
the generations before them.
Author Dan Kimball explains
the implications of the
postmodern shift for the
church and provideds practical
ideas on how it can use
worship, preaching, evangelism,
discipleship, and leadership to
reach emerging generations.

The Emerging Church
Vintage Christianity for new generations
Dan Kimball

RETAIL $16.99
ISBN 0310245648

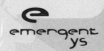

Visit **www.emergentys.com**
or your local Christian bookstore.

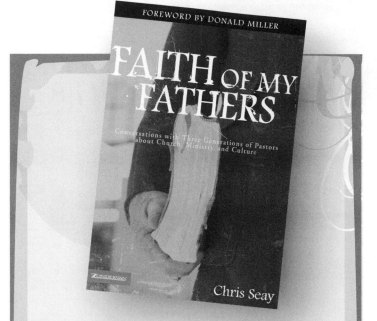

Three generations of American pastors tell their
life stories in the context of the Church. Ranging
from politics, to parenting, to UFOs—no topic
is off-limits as these passionate men articulate
what it means to nurture a missional Christianity
while loving, honoring, and embracing the
generations that have gone before.

Faith of My Fathers
Conversations with Three
Generations of Pastors about
Church, Ministry, and Culture
Chris Seay

RETAIL $16.99
ISBN 0310253268

Visit **www.youthspecialties.com** or your local Christian bookstore.

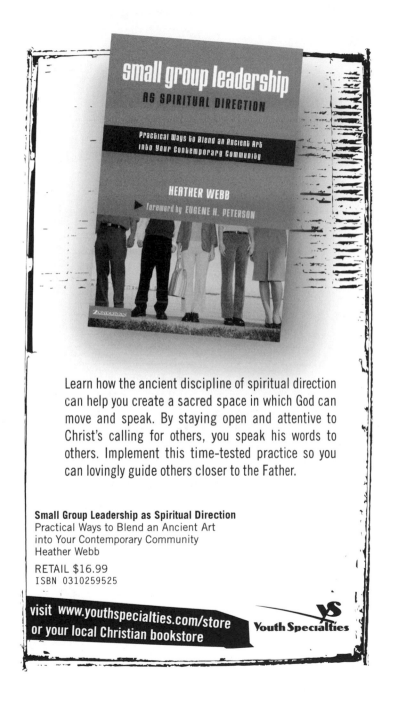

Learn how the ancient discipline of spiritual direction
can help you create a sacred space in which God can
move and speak. By staying open and attentive to
Christ's calling for others, you speak his words to
others. Implement this time-tested practice so you
can lovingly guide others closer to the Father.

Small Group Leadership as Spiritual Direction
Practical Ways to Blend an Ancient Art
into Your Contemporary Community
Heather Webb

RETAIL $16.99
ISBN 0310259525

visit **www.youthspecialties.com/store**
or your local Christian bookstore

Youth Specialties

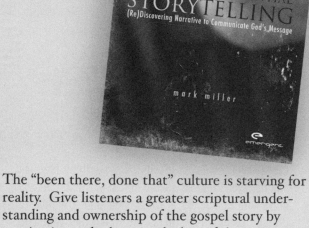

The "been there, done that" culture is starving for reality. Give listeners a greater scriptural under-standing and ownership of the gospel story by zeroing in on the hows and whys of the narrative and using hand-on experiences as innovative extensions of traditional teaching and preaching.

Eperiential Storytelling
Discovering Narrative to Communicate God's Message
Mark Miller

RETAIL $14.99
ISBN 0310255147

Visit **www.emergentys.com** or your local Christian bookstore.

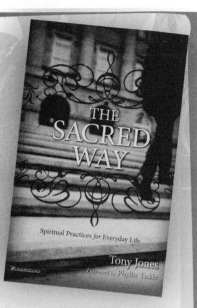

Spiritual Practices *for* Everyday Life

Tony Jones
Foreword by Phyllis Tickle

Broaden your spiritual horizons

Discover 16 ancient practices—such as the Ignatian Examen, centering prayer, and Sabbath—and learn why these proven spiritual disciplines are as relevant today as ever. Author Tony Jones briefly explores the historical and theological context of each discipline, then shows you how to implement it. If you feel like something is missing in your spiritual life, this book will challenge you to think about your relationship with God in new ways.

The Sacred Way
Spiritual Practices for Everyday Life
Tony Jones

RETAIL $12.99
ISBN 0310258103

Visit **www.emergentys.com** or your local Christian bookstore.

The Search to Belong is a practical guide for pastors and church leaders—in fact, all leaders—who struggle with building community in a culture that values belonging over believing.

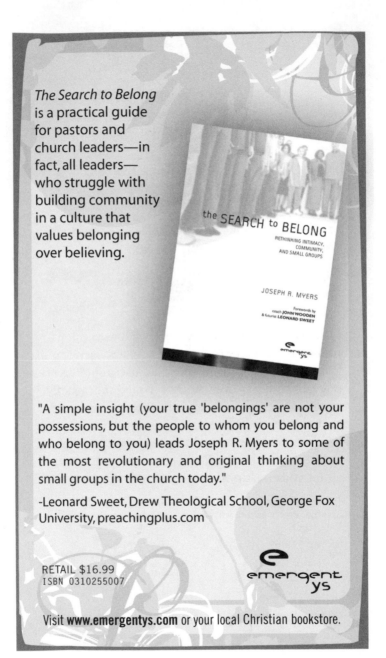

the SEARCH to BELONG

RETHINKING INTIMACY, COMMUNITY, AND SMALL GROUPS

JOSEPH R. MYERS

Forewords by
coach JOHN WOODEN
& futurist LEONARD SWEET

emergent
ys

"A simple insight (your true 'belongings' are not your possessions, but the people to whom you belong and who belong to you) leads Joseph R. Myers to some of the most revolutionary and original thinking about small groups in the church today."

-Leonard Sweet, Drew Theological School, George Fox University, preachingplus.com

RETAIL $16.99
ISBN 0310255007

emergent
ys

Visit **www.emergentys.com** or your local Christian bookstore.